PRINCIPLES OF
THE PHILOSOPHY
OF THE FUTURE

Principles of the Philosophy of the Future

Ludwig Feuerbach

Translated by
Manfred H. Vogel

Introduction by
Thomas E. Wartenberg

Hackett Publishing Company
Indianapolis/Cambridge

Ludwig Feuerbach: 1804 – 1872

Grundsätze der Philosophie der Zukunft was first published in 1843.

Cover Design by Richard L. Listenberger

For further information, please address

Hackett Publishing Company
P.O. Box 44937
Indianapolis, Indiana 46244–0937

Library of Congress Cataloging-in-Publication Data

Feuerbach, Ludwig, 1804 – 1872
    Principles of the philosophy of the future.

    Translation of: Grundsätze der Philosophie der
Zukunft.
    Reprint. Originally published: Indianapolis :
Bobbs-Merrill, c1966. With new introd.
    Bibliography: p.
    Includes index.
    1. Philosophy.   2. Religion—Philosophy.   I. Title
B2971.G72E5   1986   101   86-7699
ISBN 0-915145-26-X
ISBN 0-915145-27-8 (pbk.)

∞

Contents

v

Introduction

In the early 1840s, Ludwig Andreas Feuerbach (1804–72) published a series of books arguing that traditional religion and philosophy were radically flawed and needed to be replaced with a new form of philosophy that would inaugurate an era of human emancipation. These provocative works sparked the interest and admiration of his contemporaries. Friedrich Engels recalled that the "enthusiasm was general; we all became at once Feuerbachians"; Richard Wagner said that he "always regarded Feuerbach as the ideal exponent of the radical release of the individual from the thralldom of accepted notions"; while in England George Eliot translated *Das Wesen des Christentums,* one of Feuerbach's most important works.[1]

The reason for Feuerbach's popularity was that, in a time of social upheaval and democratic ferment, his theory held out the promise of a radical redemption of the human spirit. This redemption would take place through the elimination of those forms of consciousness— religion and philosophy—that had kept the human species from realizing its true spiritual grandeur. Feuerbach offered his contemporaries a way out of the social upheaval they felt all around them, by showing them the possibility of a new form of life in which their humanity could express itself in relations of love and affirmation.

Feuerbach's bold claims about the possibility of achieving a new form of human social life was based on his discovery that, beneath their surface, religious worship and philosophic speculation were really ways of holding the human being in thrall. Feuerbach had come to believe that God and Truth, the purported objects of religion and philosophy, were not their real objects. According to Feuerbach, when the religious person spoke of God or the philosopher discussed the

---

[1]Friedrich Engels, *Ludwig Feuerbach and the Outcome of Classical German Philosophy*, trans. C.P. Dutt (New York: International, 1941), p. 8. Richard Wagner, *My Life*. (New York: Dodd, Mead and Co., 1911,) p. 522, quoted in William J. Brazill, *The Young Hegelians* (New Haven: Yale University Press, 1970), p. 137. *The Essence of Christianity* (New York: Harper and Row, 1957) is still the only available English translation.

nature of Being and Truth, what he or she was really talking about, was the human being, only through the use of a sort of code. Feuerbach saw his task as that of exposing the nature of these codes, thereby liberating human beings from living under the illusions fostered by religion and philosophy.

In place of these systems of thought, Feuerbach proclaimed the need for an 'anthropological and materialist' philosophy, one that would begin with human beings as they concretely existed and would not posit any reality beyond that in which they lived. Without the presence of religious and philosophic abstractions, Feuerbach thought that human beings could come to realize their own divinity, thus creating a world in which the human race could fully realize its potential as a species.

Although Feuerbach's reputation underwent a rapid decline, especially among the radical thinkers of his age, his works remained an important influence on various major nineteenth- and twentieth-century thinkers. The anthropological and materialist perspective that he articulated, with its emphasis on exposing the manner in which different systems of belief can come to oppress human beings, can be seen to have left its traces in the thought of such diverse thinkers as Karl Marx, Friedrich Nietzsche, Sigmund Freud, Martin Buber, Martin Heidegger, and Jean-Paul Sartre.

Despite the historical importance of Feuerbach's thought, contemporary philosophy has paid very little attention to him. While there has been a growing awareness among American philosophers that nineteenth-century German philosophers had important things to say about the nature of the modern world, Feuerbach has remained a marginal presence. With the exception of a large body of literature on the question of his role in the development of Marxian theory, Feuerbach has been largely ignored.[2]

There are a number of reasons for this. Foremost among them, no doubt, is the nature of Feuerbach's work. For all the insightfulness of his criticisms of philosophy and religion, Feuerbach was not able to develop a positive philosophical position that adequately reflected the

---

[2]There are, of course, exceptions to this claim, a primary one being Marx Wartofsky's excellent study *Feuerbach* (Cambridge: Cambridge University Press, 1977). Feuerbach has also remained an important figure in Protestant theology.

nature of these criticisms. Feuerbach's own philosophy does not supply the revolutionary new form of thought to supplant the form of philosophical thought that Feuerbach himself claimed was inadequate for his contemporary situation. Instead, what one finds in Feuerbach is a philosophic perspective that contains the possibilities for much more far-reaching reflection and development. The very fact that Feuerbach's philosophy was influential in the development of traditions as different as Marxism, existentialism, and psychoanalysis shows that it is rich in conceptual 'raw materials.' The fertility of Feuerbach's thought as a source of inspiration for other major thinkers marks its uniqueness in the history of philosophy: No other figure in the history of thought has played so predominantly the role of muse, with the possible exception of Socrates himself.

Although it has not been as widely known to English-speaking audiences as the earlier and less mature *The Essence of Christianity*, the *Principles of the Philosophy of the Future* is one of Feuerbach's central works. The interest of this later work lies in its attempt to show that philosophy is a form of consciousness that is just as problematic as religion, standing just as much in need of a critique. In the naturalistic humanist position of the *Principles*, Feuerbach challenged the entire speculative tradition of metaphysical thought, a tradition that had ruled German philosophy and much of Western culture generally. The balance of this essay outlines Feuerbach's critique of philosophic thought and attempts to show both its richness and its limitations.

Feuerbach and the Left Hegelians

Ludwig Feuerbach was one of a number of philosophers in Germany who have come to be known as the Left Hegelians.[3] The Left Hegelians were a group of radical theologians and philosophers who articulated a thoroughgoing critique of their society by means of a critical encounter with the philosophy of Hegel. In addition to Feuer-

---

[3]John Edward Toews points out that the usual practice of calling the Right Hegelians 'Old' and the Left Hegelians 'Young' is an oversimplification of the development of Hegelianism. For this, as well as other illuminating comments on the development of the Hegelian philosophy, see his *Hegelianism, The Path Toward Dialectical Humanism, 1805 – 1841* (Cambridge: Cambridge University Press, 1980).

bach, the Left Hegelians counted among their number David Friedrich Strauss, Bruno Bauer, Arnold Ruge, Edgar Bauer, Max Stirner, and Friedrich Theodor Vischer, as well as Friedrich Engels and Karl Marx. In order to understand their philosophy, it is necessary to get a sense of the development of Hegelianism in early nineteenth-century Germany.

The importance of Hegel to the philosophical climate in which Feuerbach was raised cannot be overemphasized. Georg Wilhelm Friedrich Hegel (1770 – 1831) had attempted to systematically comprehend the entire structure and history of the world as an embodiment and realization of the logical structure of Spirit [*Geist*]. According to Hegel, this one suprahuman subject-substance, Spirit, was of such a nature that all of the developments of history and all of the diversity of the natural world could be seen to follow from it. Hegel put this point aphoristically by claiming that the real was rational, and the rational, real. Hegel's philosophic writing embodies the concrete attempt to demonstrate how the logic of Spirit can comprehend the diversity and complexity of the actual world of human experience as the rational result of historical development.

So impressive was the nature of the Hegelian synthesis that it seemed to many of Hegel's contemporaries that philosophy had virtually come to an end. In such works as the *Philosophy of Right*, Hegel had demonstrated, it appeared, that the complex structure of the human social world and its entire history could be comprehended under the single principle of the rationality of the real. The only task left for philosophy was to put the finishing touches on the grand canvas whose central landscape Hegel himself had painted.

From the beginning, however, there were competing strategies about how to finish the Hegelian synthesis. Especially during the tremendous social and political upheavals of the early decades of the century, the meaning of Hegel's comprehension of reality by the rational became a fundamental bone of contention among his followers.

One strategy adopted by Hegel's followers was that of accommodation. This camp adhered strictly to Hegel's claim to have articulated the essential structure of the one correct philosophic system in his various writings. These thinkers conceived of their task as that of continuing to fill in the gaps in his system and to bring his claims up to date, thus showing how the historical and social developments in 'reality' since his death could be accommodated within the inherent truth of the great 'rational' synthesis.

Another group of Hegel's followers was more critical of Hegel's claim to have comprehended the rational structure of the world. Although these Hegelians stood in sharp conflict with the political perspective of their more conservative counterparts, their *theoretical* disagreement with them was not very sharp. They too thought that Hegel had articulated an essentially correct philosophic method, one that could be brought to completion in their time. However, they also believed that many of Hegel's particular conclusions about the 'rational' or correct form of society and consciousness were seriously mistaken. Their position can be seen as one that affirmed the need to bring reality into accord with the rational, as opposed to the accommodationist strategy of demonstrating the rationality of existing social reality.

These critical Hegelians accounted for the discrepancy between their positive assessment of Hegel's overall philosophic position and their criticism of his particular claims about the structure of the real world and its institutions by claiming that Hegel was a victim of 'positivism,' i.e., an uncritical acceptance of the rationality of the *status quo*. They saw their task as that of exposing the uncritical—and hence irrational—side of Hegel, concealed beneath his avowedly critical philosophic position. In their very departures from his actual assertions, these Hegelians were able to claim for themselves the role of the true inheritors of the Hegelian spirit of philosophic criticism.

In the 1830s, this debate among Hegel's followers took a new and more radical form, as the truth of Hegelian philosophy itself became an issue. A number of schools of thought developed, in which different attitudes toward Hegel, and particularly toward his view of religion, were manifested. As a means of designating the spectrum of their disagreements, these schools were characterized by Strauss—one of the radical Left Hegelians—as Left, Center, and Right Hegelians.

Although the chief object of contention among these schools of Hegelian thought was religion, more was at stake in this debate than just questions of religious doctrine. Partly this is because in nine-

teenth-century Germany, questions of relgous belief had an inher-
ently social and political dimension that took on increased urgency
during the social unrest of the 1830s and 1840s. But just as important in
understanding the significance of this debate is Hegel's own understanding of Christian religion. Hegel himself had claimed that Christianity was simply an imaginative or metaphorical precursor to the
strictly conceptual knowledge contained in his philosophic system.
This was the claim the Left Hegelians contested. While their oppo-
nents argued that Christianity was, indeed, a crucial aspect of the
Hegelian system, the Left Hegelians, following the lead of Strauss,
denied this. For them, Christianity could not be reconciled with philosophic truth.

Ludwig Feuerbach was one of the central figures in the Left
Hegelian movement. Feuerbach's work contains a clear and definitive
statement of the point of view of the Left Hegelian philosophy in its
most developed form: the claim that Hegel's 'positivism' was not simply an accidental feature of the Hegelian philosophic system but
rather an essential part of its philosophic methodology. The distinctiveness of the Left Hegelian position, especially as Feuerbach
developed it, was its claim that Hegel's philosophy could *not* be the
basis of a truly critical theory of society, for it was essentially and
unalterably a form of the justification of the *status quo*.

Advancing this critical position, Feuerbach argued that the 'new
philosophy,' the 'philosophy of the future,' would have to initiate a
radical break with Hegelianism. Rather than try to expose the 'rational
core' of Hegel's system, in an attempt to bring the rest of that system
into correspondence with it, Feuerbach attempted to expose the irra-
tionality of Hegel's entire philosophic enterprise. Whereas Hegel had
claimed that his philosophy, as opposed to that of Descartes, was the
true "pathway of *doubt*, or more precisely . . . the way of despair,"
undertaking to subject all "natural" forms of "consciousness" to a
"thoroughgoing scepticism,"[4] Feuerbach argued that this is not what
the Hegelian method actually does. In the *Principles*, he claimed that
Hegel's method was one of apparent criticism only: "At first everything

[4]G.W.F. Hegel, *The Phenomenology of Spirit*, trans. A.V. Miller (Oxford: Oxford University Press, 1977), p. 49.

is overthrown, but then everything is put again in its former place; it is the same as with Descartes." [pp. 33 – 34]⁵ A truly critical philosophy, according to Feuerbach, would have to expose the deceptive nature of the Hegelian synthesis by demonstrating that it was not a philosophy of radical doubt and despair and therefore was not the truly critical philosophic theory that it claimed to be.

Despite Feuerbach's reservations about Hegel's philosophy, however, he also saw it as the logical culmination of the metaphysical tradition. In this respect, he agreed with Hegel's own claim that the importance of his philosophy resided in its role as fulfilling a certain development. Feuerbach, however, reversed the valuation of Hegel's claim by seeing Hegel's philosophy as just one more step in the process of human self-alienation rather than as its final reconciliation. What the Hegelian synthesis allowed, however, precisely because it did culminate and complete such a tradition of thought, was the possibility of overcoming that very tradition and thus actually creating the basis for the hoped-for liberation of human existence. It is this possibility that Feuerbach undertook in his own work, thus presaging the claims of Nietzsche, Heidegger, Dewey, and Wittgenstein, each of whom also claimed to be bringing the traditional form of philosophic thought to an end.⁶

The task that Feuerbach set for himself, then, is clear. He had to demonstrate that the entire history of religious and philosophic thought was a history of the development of alienated forms of human self-consciousness. Taking his cue from Kant, he would undertake a decisive *critique* of the metaphysical tradition in precisely the sense that Kant had used that word. While Feuerbach attempted to uncover the inadequate nature of the old philosophy and theology, he would at the same time found a new philosophy, based on the correct assessment of the nature of human beings that such a critique would uncover.

The importance of the *Principles of the Philosophy of the Future*, then, is that, together with the more programmatic sketches of *Necessity of a*

---

⁵All citations in brackets refer to the appropriate page of the *Principles*.
⁶These Feuerbachian themes can still be seen in Richard Rorty's interesting contemporary work, *Philosophy and the Mirror of Nature* (Princeton: Princeton University Press, 1979).

Reform of Philosophy and *Provisional Theses for the Reformation of Philosophy*, it spells out Feuerbach's conception both of the problematic nature of the Hegelian philosophy and of his own demystified—his 'new'—philosophy. In many ways Feuerbach's masterpiece, *The Essence of Christianity*, has a limited aim, viz., the critique of Christianity; it is only in the *Principles* that he goes on to expand his critical standpoint to encompass the entire metaphysical tradition of philosophy whose final development was the philosophy of Hegel.

The Essence of Christianity

In *The Essence of Christianity*, Feuerbach attempted to show that Christianity could be viewed as a form of truth. Feuerbach argued that the claims that Christianity made about God were really truths about the human species, only made in a manner that obscured this fact. Feuerbach saw Christian doctrine as essentially a code, one that he set out to decipher. The essence of the code was the positing of a being that existed apart from human beings, i.e., God, and the attribution of divinity to this being. In Feuerbach's eyes, talk of such a being was a serious mistake, one that not only mystified the nature of human existence but also degraded the human being, in as much as it glorified a nonhuman being:

Man—this is the mystery of religion—projects his being [*Wesen*] into objectivity and then again makes himself an object of this projected image of himself thus converted into a subject, a person; he thinks of himself, is an object to himself, but as the object of an object, of another being than himself.[7]

In this quotation, Feuerbach explains the two-stage process that he sees as constituting the essence of religion. First, the human being takes its self-concept and 'objectifies' this into another being, i.e., God; second, the human being sees itself as dependent on this Other, even though this Other is its own creation. Thus religion is not simply a form of consciousness in which the human being relates to another being, but it is one in which the human being conceives of itself as inferior to this Other. The critical punch of Feuerbach's claim is that it reveals the religious discussion of the nature of God to be a 'mystified'

[7]*The Essence of Christianity*, pp. 29 – 30, translation slightly modified.

way of talking about human beings. Feuerbach uses the term 'mystified' in reference to religious language because the real object of religion—the human being—is discussed by talking about a different object—God.[8]

Such an understanding of the nature of religion explains the aim of Feuerbach's philosophizing in *The Essence of Christianity*: to expose religious language for what it is, nothing but mystified claims about the human being which, properly understood, would enhance rather than demean the lives of human beings. Much of the interest of *The Essence of Christianity* lies in the demonstrations that particular religious claims about God's nature are simply obscure versions of truths about human beings. Here is one example.

> What in religion is a *predicate* we must make into a *subject*, what is a subject, into a predicate . . . that is, *invert* the oracles of religion while at the same time seizing them as counter-truths—thus do we arrive at the truth. God suffers— Suffering is the predicate—however for human beings, for others, not for himself. What does this mean in English? Nothing other than: *Suffering for others is divine*. Whoever suffers for others, who dies for them, acts divinely, is a god to human beings.[9]

This quotation provides an excellent example of Feuerbach's 'method of inversion.' Since claims about the nature of God generally involve the attribution of properties like suffering to Him, Feuerbach is able simply to invert the structure of the sentences in which they are made. The resulting sentences, instead of speaking about the nature of God as having the particular character or predicate—of suffering, in this case—will reveal the predicate itself—here, suffering—to be a divine, i.e., a valuable, characteristic of human beings. This simple and elegant 'inversion' reveals the human truth that is concealed in the religious talk about the divinity of God.

At this point, however, there seems to be an obvious problem with such a claim. After all, God is an infinite being, whereas the human being is only a finite creature. How is it possible that the claims of religion about an infinite being are really nothing but true claims about a finite being?

[8]I have employed Feuerbach's terminology in calling this a process of mystification. The terms 'reification' and 'objectification' describe aspects of this process.
[9]*The Essence of Christianity*, p. 60, translation slightly modified.

It is here that Feuerbach makes one of his most important and distinctive moves. He argues that we need to understand these claims as made, not about individual men or women, but rather about the human species as a whole. It is our 'species character' or 'species being' that is the true object of religion and theology, for the human species as a whole is infinite.[10]

Feuerbach's claim that the human species is infinite is problematic. At times, it seems that he literally means that there are no limits to what the human species can accomplish. While this is certainly hyperbole—something that, unfortunately, Feuerbach is prone to—in his more careful statements, Feuerbach is clear to specify different senses in which the human species is infinite. At one level, he says that the human species is infinite because there is no *a priori* limit that can be set either to the number of members of the species or to the range of their abilities. However, the more interesting claim that Feuerbach makes is that the human species is infinite because of its communal character, for as a species human beings are able to transcend many of the limitations that face individual finite human beings. Thus, for example, when considering the infinitude of the divine understanding, Feuerbach points out that natural science, because of its communal character, is infinite in that it allows the human species to transcend the inherent limitations on an individual's knowledge. He even argues that science, because it unites a multiplicity of finite understandings, is the realization of the very idea of an infinite understanding.[11] In this communal and anthropological decoding of religious claims about God into claims about the significance of communal human activities, Feuerbach anticipates claims made by American pragmatism about the significance of the scientific community.

For all its insightfulness, *The Essence of Christianity* remains essentially a critical work. In it, Feuerbach submits religious consciousness to a thoroughgoing critique, one that exposes the human species as the true object of religious feeling and belief. What that work did not do, however, was demonstrate that religion did not stand alone in this regard, that philosophy itself was just as much a form of mystification. Nor did it attempt to specify a new set of principles that would take the

---

[10]See, for example, *Ibid.*, p. 7 ff.
[11]He discusses this idea at some length in the *Principles*, p. 15 ff.

place of religion in a 'demystified' world, thus creating a positive, humanist consciousness. It is these tasks that set the agenda for Feuerbach's subsequent work.

The Principles of the Philosophy of the Future

The *Principles*, together with the earlier, aphoristic *Provisional Theses for the Reformation of Philosophy*, contains Feuerbach's development of his anthropological perspective into the thoroughgoing critique of philosophy that he intended to function as the basis of a truly critical philosophy that would usher in a new age for humankind. In these works, Feuerbach argues that philosophy in general and the Hegelian system in particular are concealed forms of religion and hence doubly mystified. So, if human beings are to live freely, it is as important to expose the problematic nature of philosophic speculation as to expose that of religious thought. It is this task, as well as the articulation of the framework of a 'new' form of philosophy, one free of the mystifying objectifications of the 'old' philosophy, that Feuerbach undertakes in the *Principles*.

The *Principles* can be divided into three sections, each having a specific focus. The first section (¶1 – ¶18) attempts to characterize modern philosophy as a concealed form of theology; as such, the aim of this section is to show that philosophic thought of the modern age is amenable to just the sort of critique to which Feuerbach had subjected religion in the *Essence of Christianity*. The second section (¶19 – ¶30) is an extended critique of Hegel's idealist philosophy, which Feuerbach claims marks the culmination of the modern period. Here, Feuerbach's aim is to show that Hegel's philosophy contains the seeds of its own supersession and, therefore, that there is a need to transcend it with a 'new philosophy,' the basic principles of which are presented in the third part of the *Principles* (¶31 – ¶65). Feuerbach identifies this new philosophy by a number of different terms: *empiricism, naturalism, realism, anthropologism, humanism*; in each case, these terms highlight a particular characteristic of his 'new philosophy.'

The first section of the *Principles*, then, is an attempt to show that the philosophic thought of the modern period, the old philosophy, has seen the development of an implicitly anthropological point of view:

Theology has been negated, as Feuerbach says, but as yet only from the point of view of theology. What he means by this is that the message of modern philosophy, even though framed in terms of God, is really atheism. This can be seen by considering the real innovation of modern philosophy, namely, the fundamental shift in characterizing God's nature. In earlier times, theists thought of God from the point of view of 'sensuousness,' i.e., as a sensible being, much like, though greater than, the human being; in modern times, however, speculative philosophers thought of God from the point of view of thought, i.e., in purely conceptual terms.[p. 8] Feuerbach's distinctive argument is that this really means that the actual nature of God has changed, that His existence no longer serves the same function for the modern thinker, the speculative philosopher, as it did for the theist. The ultimate result of such a development is either the pantheistic thought of Spinoza, in which God is identified with the entire natural world, or empiricism, in which God is more or less ignored. Feuerbach's startling claim is that atheism is the end result of either view: What pantheism denies in theory, i.e., that God is a being other than the world itself, empiricism denies in practice, i.e., by focusing on secular matters.[p. 22 ff.]

From a negative point of view, then, Feuerbach sees the result of the modern period of philosophy as being the formation of an atheism that needs explicit acknowledgment as such. There is more to the story than this, however, for, at the same time that modern philosophy was denying the existence of God as traditionally conceived, it was also affirming the divinity of human reason. In its reflection on God, modern philosophy was really deifying humanity, according to Feuerbach. It is in Hegel's philosophy that these dual trends of modern philosophy are fully realized.

In a number of ways, Feuerbach's treatment of the history of modern philosophy is reminiscent of Hegel's, though of course with a different thrust. Just as Hegel saw history as the story of the progress of the human race, so too Feuerbach's claims articulate a vision of history as progressive. And, again like Hegel, Feuerbach claims that the rationality of this story is concealed from its actors. Feuerbach's atheistic reading of the development of modern philosophy is the heir of Hegel's notion of the 'cunning of reason.'

When Feuerbach turns his attention to Hegel in the second part of the *Principles*, it is incumbent upon him to critique Hegel's own assessment of the significance of his thought as containing the final development of the philosophic tradition. Instead, by showing that Hegel's thought is continuous with the development of modern philosophy that he has just traced, Feuerbach intends to demonstrate the need to go beyond Hegel to his own, truly critical standpoint.

In order to accomplish this, Feuerbach seeks to show that Hegel's own systematic comprehension of reality is subject to the same sort of critical interpretation that he had given to theology itself. As we have seen, in *The Essence of Christianity* Feuerbach had argued that the mystified religious claims about God's nature were, in reality, true claims about the nature of the human being. Using this same 'method of inversion,' Feuerbach now seeks to show that even the obscure and immensely abstract claims of the Hegelian *Logic* are true so long as they are given the appropriate linguistic transformation and anthropological reinterpretation. For example, Feuerbach asks us to consider the 'unity of opposite determinations,' one of the basic principles of Hegel's philosophy. By that principle, Hegel had demanded that anyone who wanted to ascend to the heights of philosophical speculation be willing to challenge the rigid opposition between truth and falsity that is taken to characterize 'ordinary common sense.' The challenge of Hegel's philosophy was that the security of common sense would have to be rejected by anyone interested in comprehending the rational structure of reality.

Given the difficulty of the task that Hegel demanded, it is understandable that many serious students of philosophy, from Schopenhauer onwards, simply gave up, saying that it was impossible. Feuerbach, however, asks us to look more deeply into the Hegelian philosophy and to recognize that there is a veiled truth in Hegel's assertion. In order to see this truth, we need to see how it represents a feature of human experience, albeit in an obscure manner. Feuerbach's position here, as elsewhere in his writing, is remarkable for its simplicity and insight. He states:

The only means by which opposing and contradicting determinations are united in the same being in a way corresponding to reality is time . . . . The pain of contradiction consists precisely in that I am and passionately wish to be now that which in the next instant I, just as vigorously, am not and wish not to be, in that affirmation and negation follow each other, each excluding the other and each affecting me in its full determinateness and sharpness.[pp. 63 – 64]

In this passage, Feuerbach decodes the mysteries of the Hegelian system by showing that there is an easily understood interpretation of Hegel's abstract claims. Whereas Hegel had demanded that we depart from our ordinary understanding of things in order to comprehend the contradictory nature of reality, Feuerbach reinserts this 'speculative proposition' into the human context of our awareness of time, showing that there is a truth about the changeable nature of human desires concealed in Hegel's abstract philosophic truth.

Whether Feuerbach's anthropological reinterpretation of the unity of opposite determinations is adequate as a critique of Hegel is open to question. In the "Preface" to the *Phenomenology of Spirit*, Hegel himself uses an example very much like Feuerbach's, in order to show the need to develop a logic of contradiction. Indeed, it could be argued that any account of the historical genesis of the human species, including Feuerbach's own, must take some account of the 'logic' of such development, and it is precisely this 'logic' that Hegel's account of contradiction gives under the title of the unity of opposite determinations.

Be that as it may, the central element of Feuerbach's critique of Hegel in the *Principles* is the claim that Hegel's attempt to "overcome the contradiction of thought and being" is inadequate.[p. 42] In a series of insightful paragraphs, Feuerbach argues that the idealistic attempt to comprehend all of reality in thought is a sham form of comprehension that only succeeds by presupposing the outcome. Relying on Kant's distinction between $100 in thought and in reality,[12] Feuerbach argues that the distinction between thought and being is basic, something that thought must accept and not seek to transcend. Idealism is therefore an inadequate philosophical standpoint, he argues, one that can succeed only by denying the reality of the real.

This distinction is the beginning of Feuerbach's own materialist point of view, whose articulation constitutes the remainder of the *Principles*. For him, a materialist is one who accepts the 'reality of the

---

[12]100 thalers in the original. See Immanuel Kant, *Critique of Pure Reason*, trans. Norman Kemp Smith (New York: St. Martin's Press, 1929), A599/B627, p. 505.

real' as a fundamental fact that thought must come to terms with. A materialist form of philosophy must accept the derivative nature of thought, seeing it as dependent upon the nature of reality itself. Such a materialism would resist the impulse Feuerbach sees behind idealism: the attempt to go beyond the limitations of human thought and posit thought as the whole of reality.

The new philosophy that Feuerbach presents is based upon this recognition:

The new philosophy is the philosophy that thinks of the concrete not in an abstract, but in a concrete manner. It is the philosophy that recognizes the real in its reality as true . . . and raises it into the principle and object of philosophy.[p. 49]

It is with this affirmation of the 'reality of the real,' i.e., of the indispensibility of the assumption of a 'real' that is distinct from 'thought,' that Feuerbach begins the articulation of his new philosophy.

One of the central problems in Feuerbach's own philosophic position is his inability to find adequate grounds for this materialistic point of view. In the *Principles*, he makes a number of interesting attempts to ground his materialism. For example, in the discussion of Kant's example of the $100 cited earlier, Feuerbach claims that the distinguishing mark of reality is the agreement of others. In this passage and many others like it, Feuerbach seems to anticipate Wittgenstein and the pragmatists in arguing that the truth is what a community agrees upon. Feuerbach develops this idea more fully by means of his notion of the community as a fundamental relationship of an 'I' with a 'Thou,' a form that he argues is necessary to the constitution of the human being as a person.[p. 71 ff.] However, despite the originality of this idea, one that is intended as a 'this-worldly' decoding of Hegel's notion of Spirit, Feuerbach fails to develop it as the basis of an epistemology that could stand as a critical alternative to the Hegelian system.

Instead of such a 'social epistemology,' Feuerbach gives us another account of the nature of reality, one according to which the real is that which is given through sensation: "The real in its reality or taken as real is the real as an object of the senses; it is the sensuous."[p. 51] Aligning himself with the traditional empiricist claim that sensation is the mark of the real, Feuerbach argues that this entails that space and time are forms of reality itself, "laws of existence as well as of thought."[p. 60] His point is that human access to reality is conditioned by the structure of reality itself, that we cannot form the concept of an object that is not conditioned by a sensible nature. It is the nature of reality which determines the structure of our thought.

Feuerbach uses this view to argue against the meaningfulness of Hegel's speculative propositions in a manner foreshadowing the claims of twentieth-century logical positivism.[p. 51 ff., p. 60 ff.] Feuerbach's account of how sensation reflects the reality of the real is, at best, suggestive, however, for once again we find him shifting ground rather than developing his insights more fully. Relying on the ambiguity of the notion of the sensuous, Feuerbach presents a third version of materialism: that feeling [*Empfindung*] is the key to reality.

The role of feelings in structuring our understanding of reality is a characteristic Feuerbachian theme. Feuerbach already argued that the conception of the human being articulated by modern thought was an abstract and disembodied one, one that privileged reason over other human capacities, such as action and emotion.[See pp. 30 – 31] This was an important aspect of his critique of modern philosophy, for he claimed that the 'reason' that modern philosophy saw present in the world was nothing but the objectified form of the philosopher's actual life. The philosophers who led lives in which reason was itself dominant over feelings and actions simply projected the structure of their own lives onto the world.

In the present context, Feuerbach extends this claim by arguing that the new philosophy needs to accord a greater importance to feelings in general and to love in particular.

Hence, human feelings . . . have ontological and metaphysical significance . . . . there is no other proof of being but love and feeling in general. That object whose being affords you pleasure and whose nonbeing affords you pain—that alone exists.[p. 53]

The attempt to incorporate other aspects of the human being into our conception both of our natures and of the world itself is certainly an important philosophic innovation. It enables us to see the failure of modern thought to treat emotions as cognitively significant. This idea is one that was taken up by the existentialists and is again being heard today in the claims of the deconstructivists; it shows Feuerbach as an innovative critic of traditional thought.

Feuerbach's various attempts to ground the new philosophy in a form of materialism are both innovative and suggestive. A central weakness of Feuerbach's thought is that it elides the differences between distinct senses of materialism, rather than providing an account of their interrelations. Feuerbach slips comfortably from one to the next, relying on the verbal identity which his multiple uses of the term 'materialism' permits.

Our discussion of the ambiguities in Feuerbach's materialism can help us see why Feuerbach's positive thought has not been as influential as his criticisms of religion and philosophy. Feuerbach's critiques of traditional thought give the reader a sense of a new possibility for human life, one in which the power of such mystified forms of thought to structure and limit the lives of human beings has been undercut. His critique of traditional forms of thought is like a breath of fresh air, giving us a glimpse of the possibility of throwing off our intellectual chains. Feuerbach's own positive philosophy, however, seems unable to handle the difficult task of providing a successor to the tradition whose weaknesses he himself was pivotal in exposing: It does not provide an adequate ground for a way of life lived 'beyond religion and philosophy.' The themes of his own theory call for such a development, but it was left to philosophers other than Feuerbach to continue along those paths he had been the first to tread.

Thus Feuerbach's 'new philosophy,' while conceived of as an overcoming of traditional philosophy, fails to achieve the break with traditional theorizing that he had himself demanded. While Feuerbach was one of the first to attempt to overcome philosophy itself, he was not able to divorce himself from the tradition of philosophy fully enough to put forward a theory that truly was 'in a new key.' Though he was an inspiration to theorists from Marx to Heidegger, unlike theirs, his 'new' philosophy was unable to fill the space he had created for it.

Feuerbach's Critical Method

Having explored the nature of Feuerbach's claims in the *Principles*, we should now consider the importance of his philosophy from a more general point of view. One genuine contribution that Feuerbach made to the philosophic tradition is worth considering, namely, a new conception of philosophic method and argumentation: the genetico-critical method.

Feuerbach's methodology is worth exploring in some detail, for it marks a break with a good deal of traditional philosophic writing. For many modern philosophers, philosophical statements were conceptualized primarily as assertions, that is, propositions that make a claim to truth. The appropriate mode for challenging such claims was to prove that they were incoherent or false. Thus, to choose one outstanding example of this method, Berkeley shows over and over again that Locke's claim that material substance exists is riddled with contradictions and hence needs to be rejected.[13] As a result, Berkeley establishes his own theory of spiritual substances by this method of indirect proof.

Although Feuerbach does use this form of argument to show that certain claims made by theology are contradictory—for example, in the second part of *The Essence of Christianity*—it is more characteristic of him to use a different, more radical means of refuting a theory with which he disagrees. He characterizes this other method as the genetico-critical method, and it constitutes a lasting philosophic innovation that influenced many philosophers.

The use of a 'genetic' method in philosophy can be traced back to John Locke in *An Essay Concerning Human Understanding*.[14] In that work, Locke argued that no idea present in the human mind could be used with justification as a description of reality unless it was possible to demonstrate the origin of that idea in human experience. Thus, Locke was able to demonstrate that ideas like that of an apple had a legitimate employment because they could be resolved into component ideas, in this case red, round, and sweet, all of which were presented together in sensory experience. On the other hand, since an idea like that of a centaur, although itself perhaps composed of sensible ideas, did not itself get presented in experience, its use could not be justified.[15]

One aspect of the genetic method that Locke did not fully develop was its use as a powerful tool for the criticism of traditional philo-

---

[13]See, for example, his *Three Dialogues between Hylas and Philonous*, ed. Robert M. Adams (Indianapolis: Hackett, 1979).

[14]New York: Dover Publications, 1959. See especially Book II.

[15]*Ibid.*, Bk. II, Ch. xxx, ¶ 5.

sophic doctrines. In the hands of a skillful dialectician, it could be used to criticize not simply the truth of a philosophic theory but also the meaningfulness of the terms in which that theory was articulated. David Hume's philosophy contains an attempt to use this method to show that all the central ideas of traditional metaphysics—from causality to personal identity—do not have a legitimate employment, since they are not derivable from sense experience.[16]

This method had fallen into disuse in Germany for a number of reasons. Primary among them was Kant's dismissal of the Lockean genetic method in the *Critique of Pure Reason*. Distinguishing between a question of fact and a question of justification,[17] Kant argued that the Lockean genetic method was not valid; just because an idea was not derived from experience did not mean that it could not be shown to have a legitimate use in the realm of experience. Indeed, Kant's own revolutionary transcendental method is aimed at showing the necessity of using metaphysical concepts that are not capable of a Lockean abstraction from experience.

When we turn to Feuerbach's own methodolgy, we find him using a method that seems very much related to Locke's. Feuerbach's genetic-critical method is not, however, a simple reversion to the standpoint of pre-Kantian empiricism. In common with Locke, Feuerbach is not concerned to criticize his opponent's view in regard to the truth or falsity of their claims, but rather to question the terms in which the claims are made. In Feuerbach's case, however, this involves asking a question somewhat different from Locke's, namely, *What need of the human heart is being satisfied by a particular philosophic doctrine?*

The real thrust of this radical move is that it sees even the most abstract form of philosophic and religious thought as unwittingly betraying its origins in the concrete emotional life of the human being. It is this stance that rationalizes Feuerbach's critical account of religion and philosophy. We have already seen that Feuerbach claims that there is a veiled attempt to understand the nature of human beings contained behind the explicit content of theology and philosophy.

[16]See, for example, David Hume, *A Treatise on Human Nature*, ed. L.A. Selby-Bigge (Oxford: Oxford University Press, 1888).

[17]Kant, *Ibid.*, A84/B116, p. 120.

The objectifying language of religious and philosophic texts, however, obscured this fact by talking of God and Being. These putative objects are, however, nothing but false projections of the nature of the human species, which Feuerbach refers to as 'man,'[18] The 'genetico-critical' method Feuerbach uses is one that seeks to show the needs that such belief fulfills for people, rather than to argue about their truth. For example, when Feuerbach asks. ". . . for where else than in the pains and needs of man does this being who is without pain and without needs [i.e., God] have its ground and origin?"[p. 48] Feuerbach is showing the origins of the idea of God in a particular desire that human beings have, i.e., the desire to live a life free from the painful nature of their needy existence; he does not demonstrate the logical inadequacies of a particular attempt to prove God's existence. The significance of this type of critical argument is that it does not simply concentrate on a particular formulation of a claim about God or Being, but allows us to understand the reasons that a theologian or philosopher actually would have for advancing such a view in the first place.

This 'genetico-critical method' is one of Feuerbach's true philosophic innovations. It asks us to realize that the claims that certain ideas and concepts make about the world are but a superficial level of the 'meaning' of these ideas and concepts, one that conceals a deeper level where these ideas serve a function within the experience of human beings. In different ways, Marx, Nietzsche, and Freud all understood this aspect of Feuerbach's philosophy and used it to advantage in their own theories.

This aspect of Feuerbach's thought has been one of its most controversial. Although it has been criticized as a form of the 'genetic fallacy,' i.e., the assumption that exposing the origin of an idea has any relevance to the ultimate validity of it, such a criticism ultimately is wide of the mark. The importance of Feuerbach's innovation is that it lets us see that ideas are more than attempts to mirror the structure of the

---

[18]Feuerbach's use of the term 'man' is not as sexist as it might seem. The German term is *Mensch*. In *The Essence of Christianity*, [Ch. 10], he goes on to stress the importance of genders: "The human being [*Mensch*], however, exists only as man [*Mann*] and woman [*Weib*]." Eliot's translation obscures this point. Feuerbach's use of the term 'man' is thus often specifically generic.

world, that they function within the life-context of the human being in a way that is important to the assessment of their validity.

A Critical Assessment

In conclusion, a few general comments about the nature of Feuerbach's philosophy are in order. Feuerbach's anthropological standpoint is both the great strength and the fatal flaw of his materialism and humanism: important because it enables him to assess the whole tradition of modern European philosophy in a fundamentally new way and to attempt to overturn it, but also problematic in that the basis of that perspective in the concept of 'man' or of the 'human community' is itself an objectification. While he criticizes previous philosophic theories for the objectified forms of being that they posit, Feuerbach never turns his own critical glance upon himself. He lacks a critical perspective from which to see that neither 'man' nor 'community' is a term sufficiently concrete to explain the varied and specific ways in which human life is shaped by differing social environments.[19]

Thus, Feuerbach's conception of human sociality remains an abstract one. Although he speaks, for example, of heterosexual love as the true form of community, he does not seem to recognize that the form in which such love is embodied will vary depending upon historical and social circumstances. The irony here is that the very standpoint that allows Feuerbach to see the limitations of Hegel's philosophy blind him to one of Hegel's great insights, namely, that human beings assume a specific character as a result of the specific structure of social relations they have with other human beings.[20] For all the abstraction of his idealist metaphysics, Hegel's attempt to explicate the nature of human life does more justice to our sociality and its historically varied character than does Feuerbach's avowedly communitarian and materialist perspective. The task that Marx set for himself—

---

[19]In his later work, such as the *Lectures on the Essence of Religion*, trans. Ralph Manheim (New York: Harper and Row, 1967), Feuerbach does criticize his anthropologism, but the naturalism he advocates there does not solve the problems discussed in this essay.

[20]For an example of this, consider the different theoretical concepts—person, subject, etc.—that Hegel uses to refer to concrete individuals in the *Philosophy of Right*, trans. T.M. Knox (Oxford: Oxford University Press, 1952).

synthesizing the insights of these two philosophers—begins from this insight.

One of the problems here may be a certain self-satisfaction in Feuerbach's thought. In his attempt to demonstate that religion and philosophy are forms of human self-alienation, Feuerbach fails to fully answer one very significant question, namely, why such a self-alienation is necessary. The story he tells, for all its persuasiveness, remains strange and troubling. That human beings should invent a fantastic world in order to reflect upon the one they themselves inhabit and that this object should take the form of a Divine Being or even of Being itself is something that Feuerbach seeks to reveal. He fails, however, to provide a systematic answer to the question of why such a peculiar process of self-knowledge is necessary for the human being. In other words, the question of what it is about the human being that compels it to deny its own nature via the abstractions of a godhead or metaphysics is an issue that Feuerbach not only fails to adequately resolve but even evades by entitling it a mystery.[21] And, though he does say that such forms of objectivity arise from the needs of the subject, he never pushes himself to account for the peculiar nature of this process of alienation and objectification. Confronted with an historical theory in the form of Hegel's idealist metaphysics, Feuerbach took refuge in an ahistorical materialism that is ultimately unsatisfactory.

In this sense, Feuerbach's own romantic optimism about the human species may be the cause of the failure. His need to affirm the nature of the human being in the face of the huge self-deprecations of the onto-theological tradition blinds him to the possibility that human nature is of a darker sort than he imagined. Both Nietzsche and Freud take up from where Feuerbach left off, developing views about the human being that recognize the importance of a 'darker side.'[22]

[21]See page xiv above. Freud's theory of religion marks a distinct advance upon Feuerbach in that (i) Freud seeks to show how the idea of a god is derived from specific features of childhood experience, and (ii) the theory of the unconscious explains why certain ideas cannot be thought about directly, and therefore do require a sort of code. See, for example, his *Future of an Illusion*, trans. James Strachey (New York: W.W. Norton & Co., 1928). It should be noted that Feuerbach's sympathy for religion allows him to do more justice to its positive functions than Freud is able to.

[22]In particular, it is interesting to contrast their views on the nature of religion with Feuerbach's. As well as Freud, *Ibid.*, see Nietzsche, *The Anti-Christ*, in Walter Kaufmann, *The Portable Nietzsche* (Harmondworth: Penguin Books Ltd., 1968).

As a consequence of these inadequacies, Feuerbach's conception of human emancipation is just as abstract as his notion of community. Although he claims that he is interested in the practical emancipation of human beings, he remains wedded to the idea that such emancipation will be the natural outcome of the theoretical emancipation he believed his own philosophy to embody. His emancipatory discourse of a practical liberation of humanity is thus highly problematic, a fact that Marx was quick to recognize and criticize.[23]

Despite these limitations, Feuerbach's thought is fertile ground for serious philosophical reflection. His critique of religious and philosophic abstractions provides a stimulating and enriching vision of human life freed from the limitations of inherited forms of thought and feeling. In many ways, even the limitations of Feuerbach's thought make it an exciting object for a critical encounter. In his work, there are deep and stimulating reflections on the nature of human existence, but reflections that one feels impelled to push further, to develop in different directions. Being the stimulus to original philosophic reflection is, after all, one of the most important roles that a philosopher can play, and it is a role for which Ludwig Feuerbach is still eminently suited.[24]

Thomas E. Wartenberg
Mount Holyoke College

---

[23]See his well-known "Theses on Feuerbach," reprinted, for example, in Robert C. Tucker, *The Marx-Engels Reader* (New York: W.W. Norton & Co., Inc., 1978), pp. 143–145. But see also Marx Wartofsky's claim that Marx's critique of Feuerbach ignores Feuerbach's psychological insights, so that the solution to conflict between them is still unresolved (*Ibid.*, p. 225).

[24]This essay has benefitted from the comments of friends and colleagues. I would especially like to thank Alan Schiffmann and John Grayson for their insightful comments and encouragement.

Selected Bibliography

Complete Works

Feuerbach's complete works are available in two editions. The first is a thirteen-volume set edited by Hans-Martin Sass, entitled *Sämmtliche Schriften* (Stuttgart: Frommann-Holzboog) 1960 – 1964. It is a reprint, with some supplementary volumes, of the Bolin-Jodl edition of the *Sämmtliche Werke* (Stuttgart: Frommann Verlag), 1903 – 1910. The second is a new, critical edition edited by Werner Schuffenhauer, entitled *Gesammelte Werke* (Berlin: Akademie-Verlag) 1967 – . It will consist of sixteen volumes when completed.

Works by Feuerbach in English

The Essence of Christianity. Translated by George Eliot. New York: Harper, 1957. The classic translation of Feuerbach's most famous work, with an interesting introductory essay by Karl Barth on Feuerbach's relation to Protestant theology.

The Fiery Brook: Selected Writings of Ludwig Feuerbach. Translated by Zawar Hanfi. New York: Doubleday, 1972. A selection of a number of different texts by Feuerbach.

Lectures in the Essence of Religion. Translated by Ralph Mannheim. New York: Harper and Row, 1967. A late work in which Feuerbach continues the program of *The Essence of Christianity*. He argues here that religion originates in the human feeling of dependency upon nature.

Provisional Theses for the Reformation of Philosophy and *Towards a Critique of Hegelian Philosophy*, in *The Left Hegelians: An Anthology*. Edited by

Lawrence C. Stepelvitch. London: Cambridge University Press, 1983. This volume contains a number of interesting works by other Left Hegelians, as well as these important texts by Feuerbach.

Thoughts on Death and Immortality. Translated by James A. Massey. Berkeley: University of California Press, 1980. An early work, for which Feuerbach was relieved of his teaching duties. In it, Feuerbach argues against the idea of personal immortality.

Works on Feuerbach in English

Althusser, Louis. *For Marx*. Translated by Ben Brewster. London: New Left Books, 1977. Althusser's attempt to 'excise' any Feuerbachian influence on the 'mature' Marx has been the focus of much recent discussion of Marx's relation to Feuerbach.

Brazill, William J. *The Left Hegelians*. New Haven: Yale Unversity Press, 1970. The chapter on Feuerbach gives a good general overview of his life and work, although the *Principles* is not discussed.

Chamberlain, William B. *Heaven Wasn't His Destination: The Philosophy of Ludwig Feuerbach*. London: George Allen and Unwin, 1941. A clear general examination of Feuerbach's philosophy, containing an interesting discussion of Feuerbach's influence on German literature.

Colletti, Lucio. *Marxism and Hegel*. Translated by Lawrence Garner. London: New Left Books, 1973. Contains an innovative, but contentious discussion of Feuerbach's Kantianism and its role in the formation of Marx's thought.

Engels, Friedrich. "Ludwig Feuerbach and the End of Classical German Philosophy," in Karl Marx and Friedrich Engels, *Selected Works*. New York: International, 1968. The standard account of Feuerbach's influence on Marx.

Kamenka, Eugene. *The Philosophy of Ludwig Feuerbach*. New York: Praeger, 1970. A highly readable and informative account of Feuerbach's philosophy. Gives a good account of his life and philosophical development.

Löwith, Karl. *From Hegel to Nietzsche*. Translated by David Green. New York: Doubleday, 1967. The classic study of the development of the philosophy of this period, containing many important observations on Feuerbach's place in this history.

Marx, Karl, and Engels, Friedrich. *The German Ideology*. Edited by C.J. Arthur. New York: International, 1970. Contains an extended critique of Feuerbach, as well as the famous *Theses on Feuerbach*.

McLellan, David. *The Left Hegelians and Karl Marx*. New York: Praeger, 1969. A very readable study of the Left Hegelians that focuses on Marx's relation to Feuerbach and the other Left Hegelians.

Sass, Hans-Martin, ed. *Feuerbach, Marx, and the Left Hegelians*. *Philosophical Forum*, Volume VIII, Nos. 2 – 4, 1978. An impressive collection of essays that includes translations of some short works by Feuerbach and a number of provocative assessments of his work by contemporary philosophers.

Schnädelbach, Herbert. *Philosophy in Germany* 1833 – 1933. London: Cambridge University Press, 1983. Provides a good general account of the intellectual context in which Feuerbach worked. Not much material on Feuerbach himself.

Toews, John Edward. *Hegelianism: The Path Toward Dialectical Humanism*, 1805 – 1841. Cambridge: Cambridge University Press, 1980. An impressive scholarly study that attempts to correct the traditional picture of the development of Hegelianism, which has focused almost exclusively on the transition to Marx. Includes interesting discussions of Feuerbach and his relation to Strauss and Bauer.

Wartofsky, Marx. *Feuerbach*. Cambridge: Cambridge University Press, 1977. A detailed and scholarly study of Feuerbach. The standard work in the field. It relates Feuerbach's own philosophical development to the content of his theories in a genuinely informative manner. It makes the case for treating Feuerbach seriously as a philosopher.

PRINCIPLES OF
THE PHILOSOPHY OF
THE FUTURE

Preface to the First Edition

These principles contain the continuation and further justification of my *Thesen zur Reform der Philosophie*, which was banned by the most arbitrary decree of the German censors. According to the first manuscript, these principles were intended to lead to a detailed book; but, when I reached the phase of making a fine copy, I was seized—I myself do not know how—by the spirit of the German censors, and I cut it like a barbarian. What remained from this indiscreet censorship was reduced to the following few pages.

I called them *Principles of the Philosophy of the Future* because generally the present era, as an era of refined illusions and priggish prejudices, is incapable of understanding, not to speak of appreciating, the simple truths from which these principles are abstracted—precisely because of their simplicity.

The philosophy of the future has the task of leading philosophy from the realm of "departed souls" back into the realm of embodied and living souls; of pulling philosophy down from the divine, self-sufficient bliss in the realm of ideas into human misery. To this end, it needs nothing more than human understanding and human speech. To think, speak, and act in a pure and true human fashion will, however, be granted only to future generations. At present, the task is not to present man as such, but to pull him out of the mud in which he has been embedded. These principles are the fruit of this unsavory work of cleansing. The task of these principles was to derive the necessity of a philosophy of man, that is, of anthropology, from the philosophy of the absolute, that is, theology, and to establish the critique of human philosophy through the critique of divine philosophy. Thus, these principles presuppose, for their evaluation, a close familiarity with the philosophy of the modern era.

The consequences of these principles will certainly follow.

Bruckberg
July 9, 1843

Principles of the
Philosophy of the Future

1

The task of the modern era was the realization and humanization of God—the transformation and dissolution of theology into anthropology.

2

The religious or practical form of this humanization was Protestantism. The God who is man, the human God, namely, Christ—only this is the God of Protestantism. Protestantism is no longer concerned, as Catholicism is, about what God is in himself, but about what he is for man; it has, therefore, no longer a speculative or contemplative tendency, as is the case in Catholicism. It is no longer theology; it is essentially Christology, that is, religious anthropology.

3

God in himself, or God as God—for God in himself is only then essentially God—was, however, negated by Protestantism only in a practical way; theoretically, it left him untouched. He exists, but not for the religious man. He is a transcendent being that will become an object for man only when he is in Heaven. But what lies in the other world for religion lies in this world for philosophy; what is no object for the former is precisely the object for the latter.

4

Speculative philosophy is the rational or theoretical elaboration and dissolution of God, who is, for religion, other-worldly.

5

The essence of speculative philosophy is nothing but the rationalized, realized, presented essence of God. Speculative philosophy is the true, consistent, and rational theology.

6

God as God—as an intellectual or abstracted being, that is, a nonhuman, nonsensuous being that is an object only of reason or intelligence and is accessible only to them—is nothing but the essence of reason itself. He is, however, conceived by ordinary theology or theism by means of the imagination as a being distinct from and independent of reason. It is, therefore, an intrinsic and holy necessity that the essence of reason —which is now separated from it—be finally identified with reason, that the divine being be recognized as the being of reason and be realized and presented as such. On this necessity rests the paramount historical significance of speculative philosophy.

The proof that the divine being is the being of reason or of intellect lies in the fact that the determinations or attributes of God—insofar, of course, as they are rational or intellectual —are not determinations of sensation or of the imagination, but attributes of reason.

"God is the infinite being, the being without any limitation." But that which is not a boundary or a limit for God is also not a limit for reason. Where, for instance, God is a being elevated above the limits of sensation, there also, surpassing those limits, is reason. Whoever can think of no other being but a sensuous being, whoever therefore possesses a reason limited by sensation, will, precisely as a result, also have a God limited by sensation. That reason that conceives of God as an unlimited being conceives of God only its own limitlessness. That which is a divine being for reason is also the truly reasonable being for it—that is, the being that is completely congruent with reason and, therefore, precisely satisfies it. However, that in which a being finds its satisfaction is nothing other than its objectified being. He who satisfies himself through a poet is himself of a poetic nature; he who satisfies himself through a philosopher is himself of a philosophical nature; and the fact that he is this becomes only in the moment of satisfaction an object for him and others. Reason, "however, does not stop at sensuous and finite objects; it satisfies itself only in the infinite being." Thus, the essence of reason is disclosed to us only in this being.

"God is necessary being." But his necessity rests on the fact that he is a rational, intelligent being. The world, that is, matter, does not contain the cause of its being nor of the way it exists in itself; the world is completely indifferent to whether it exists, to whether it exists thus or otherwise.[1] Thus, the world necessarily presupposes another being as cause and, indeed, an understanding, a self-conscious being that acts according to reasons and purposes. For, if intelligence is taken away from this other being, the question is raised anew as to its cause. The necessity of the primary, highest being rests, therefore, on the presupposition that the understanding alone is the primary, highest, necessary, and true being. Just as, in general, the metaphysical or ontotheological determinations first assume truth and reality when they are traced back to psychological or, rather, anthropological determinations, so also the necessity of the divine being in the old metaphysics or ontotheology first assumes meaning and understanding, truth and reality, in the psychological or anthropological determination of God as an intelligent being. The necessary being is the being that necessitates its being thought, that is

---

[1] It is self-understood that here, as in all other sections where historical material is involved and developed, I do not speak and argue from my point of view, but rather in the name of the historical point of view represented. Thus, here I speak for theism.

simply affirmed, simply undeniable or indestructible—but only as a self-thinking being. In this necessary being, therefore, reason proves and demonstrates only its own necessity and reality.

"God is unconditional, general—'God is not this or that' —immutable, eternal, or timeless being." But absoluteness, immutability, eternity, and generality are themselves, according to the judgment of metaphysical theology, also attributes of the truths or laws of reason, consequently attributes of reason itself; for what are these unalterable, general, unconditioned truths of reason that are valid always and everywhere if not expressions of the essence of reason?

"God is independent, self-sufficient being who needs no other being for his own being, consequently existing by and through himself." But here, too, this abstract, metaphysical determination has meaning and reality only as a definition of the essence of reason and states, therefore, nothing but that God is a thinking, intelligent being or conversely that only a thinking being is divine; for only a sensuous being needs other, external objects for its being. I do need air in order to breathe, water to drink, light to see, vegetable and animal materials to eat; but nothing, at least directly, in order to think. I cannot conceive of a breathing being without air, a seeing being without light, but I can conceive of a thinking being isolated in itself. That being that breathes necessarily relates itself to a being external to itself and has its essential object through which it is what it is outside itself; but a thinking being relates to itself, being its own object, having its essence in itself, and being what it is through itself.

7

That which is object in theism is subject in speculative philosophy; what in the former is only the conceived and imagined being of reason is in the latter the thinking being of reason itself.

The theist conceives God as an existing and personal being

external to reason and in general apart from man; he, as subject, thinks about God as an object. He conceives God as a being; namely, according to his imagination, God is a spiritual and unsensuous being, but, in accordance with actuality, that is, with the truth, he is a sensuous being; for the essential characteristic of an objective being, of a being outside thoughts or the imagination, is sensation. He distinguishes God from himself in the same way in which he distinguishes sensuous objects and beings as existing apart from him; in short, he conceives God from the point of view of sensation. The speculative theologian or philosopher, on the other hand, conceives God from the point of view of thought. He therefore does not have the disturbing appearance of a sensuous being midway between him and God. He thus identifies, without any hindrance, the objective, conceived being with the subjective, thinking being.

The intrinsic necessity by which God changes from an object of man to his subject, to his thinking ego, can be derived more precisely from that which was already expounded in the following way. God is an object of man, and only of man; he is not an object of animals. The essence of a being is recognized, however, only through its object; the object to which a being is necessarily related is nothing but its own revealed being. Thus, the object of herbivorous animals is the plant; however, by means of this object they essentially differentiate themselves from the other animals, the carnivorous ones. Thus, the object of the eye is neither tone nor smell, but light. In the object of the eye, however, its essence is revealed to us. It is, therefore, irrelevant whether one cannot see or does not possess an eye. We therefore also name in life things and beings only according to their objects. The eye is "the light organ." He who cultivates the soil is a farmer; he who makes hunting the object of his activity is a hunter; he who catches fish is a fisherman; and so on. If, now, God is an object of man—and, indeed, inasmuch as he really is a necessary and essential object—what is expressed in the being of this object is merely the peculiar essence of man. Imagine to yourself a thinking being on a planet or even a comet seeing a few paragraphs of Christian dogmatics dealing with the being of God. What would this being conclude from these paragraphs? Perhaps the existence of a god in the sense of Christian dogmatics? No! it would infer only that there are thinking beings also on earth; it would find in the definitions of the earth inhabitants regarding their god only definitions of their own being. For example, in the definition 'God is a spirit' it would find only the proof and expression of their own spirit; in short, the essence and attributes of the subject would be derived from the essence and attributes of the object. And rightly so, for the distinction between what the object is in itself and what it is for man is removed in the case of this object. This distinction is only justifiable in the case of a directly sensed object, which is precisely, therefore, an object also of beings apart from man. Light exists not only for man, but it affects also animals, plants, and inorganic substances: it is a general entity. In order to find what light is, we consider, therefore, not only its impact and effects on us, but also on other beings distinct from us. The distinction between the object in itself and the object for us—namely, between the object in reality and the object in our thought and imagination—is therefore necessarily and objectively grounded here. God is, however, only an object of man. Animals and stars praise God only in the mind of man. It is, thus, an innate characteristic of God's own essence that he is an object of no being other than man, that he is a specifically human object, a secret of man. But, if God is only an object of man, what is revealed to us in his essence? Nothing but the essence of man. That whose object is the highest being is itself the highest being. The more of man animals assume as an object, the higher they rank and the closer they approach man. An animal whose object were man as man, the essential human being, would no longer be an animal but itself man. Only equal beings—and, indeed, as they are in themselves—are objects for one another. The identity of the divine and human being is, to be sure, known also to theism. But, because the theist conceives God as a sensuous being existing apart from man—disregarding the fact that at the same time he places the essence of God in the spirit—this identity is for him also an object, but only as a sensuous identity, as similarity or kinship. Kinship expresses the same relationship as identity; but at the same time kinship is bound to the sensuous imagination by which the related beings are made into two independent, that is, sensuous, beings existing apart from each other.

8

Ordinary theology transforms the point of view of man into the point of view of God; speculative theology, on the other hand, transforms the point of view of God into the point of view of man or, rather, of the thinker.

For ordinary theology, God is an object and, indeed, an object just like any other sensuous object; but, at the same time, he is also for ordinary theology a subject, just like the human subject. God creates things that are apart from him, relates himself to himself and to other beings that exist apart from him, loves and thinks himself and other beings at the same time. In short, man transforms his thoughts and even his emotions into thoughts and emotions of God, his essence and his viewpoint into the essence and viewpoint of God. Speculative theology, however, reverses this. Hence, in ordinary theology, God is self-contradictory, for he is supposed to be a nonhuman and superhuman being; yet in truth he is—according to all his determinations—a human being. In speculative theology or philosophy, on the other hand, God is in contradiction to man; he is supposed to be the essence of man, at least of reason, and yet in truth he is a nonhuman and superhuman, that is, abstracted being. In ordinary theology, the superhuman God is only imaginary, an edifying cliché and a toy of fantasy; in speculative philosophy, on the other hand, he is truth and bitter seriousness. The severe contradiction in which speculative philosophy became involved was caused only by the fact that it made God—who in theism is only a being of fantasy, a far-removed, indefinite, and cloudy being—into a present and definite being, thus destroying the illusive charm that a being far removed has in the blue haze of the imagination. Thus, the theists were much upset over the fact that, according to Hegel, logic is supposed to be the presentation of God in his eternal, preworldly essence, and yet, for example, in the section on quantity, it deals with extensive and intensive quantity, fractions, powers, and proportions. What, they cried out, should this God be our God? And yet this God is nothing but the God of theism who is drawn out of the fog of the indefinite imagination into the light of definite thought, the God of theism, so to speak, taken at his word of having created and ordered everything according to measure, number, and weight. If God has ordered and created all according to quantity and measure, then measure and quantity before they were realized in things existing apart from God were—and still are—in the mind and consequently in the essence of God, for there is no difference between the mind of God and his essence. Does, then, mathematics not also belong to the mysteries of theology? But, of course, a being appears quite different in fancy and imagination than in truth and reality; no wonder that one and the same being appears to those who only follow mere appearance and semblance as two completely distinct beings.

9

The essential attributes or predicates of the divine being are the essential attributes or predicates of speculative philosophy.

10

God is pure spirit, pure essence, and pure action (*actus purus*), without passion, external determination, sensation, or matter. Speculative philosophy is this pure spirit and pure activity realized as an act of thought—the absolute being as absolute thought.

By the same token that abstraction from all that is sensuous and material was once the necessary condition of theology, so was it also the necessary condition of speculative philosophy, except for the difference that the theological abstraction was, as it were, a sensuous abstraction, because its object, although reached by abstraction, was at the same time imagined as a sensuous being, whereas the abstraction of speculative philosophy is an intellectual and ideated abstraction that has only scientific or theoretical, but not practical, meaning. The beginning of Descartes' philosophy, namely, the abstraction from sensation and matter, is the beginning of modern speculative philosophy. However, Descartes and Leibniz considered this abstraction merely as a subjective condition in order to know the immaterial, divine being; they conceived the immateriality of God as an objective attribute independent of abstraction and thought; they still shared the viewpoint of theism in conceiving the immaterial being only as an object, but not as a subject, as the active principle and real essence of philosophy. To be sure, God is also in Descartes and Leibniz the principle of philosophy, but only as an object distinct from thought and therefore a principle only in general and in the imagination, but not in actuality and truth. God is only the prime and general cause of matter, motion, and activity; but particular motions and activities and specific, real, and material objects are considered and known as independent of God. Leibniz and Descartes are idealists only in general, but specifically they are materialists. Only God is the consistent, complete, and true idealist, for only he conceives all things without obscurity, that is, without the senses and the imagination (according to the meaning of Leibniz' philosophy). He is pure mind, that is, mind that is separated from all that is sensuous and material; material things are for him, therefore, pure entities of the mind and pure thought-objects; for him, matter does not exist at all, because it rests on obscure, that is, sensuous conceptions. But, at the same time, man, too, in Leibniz' philosophy, has already in himself a good portion of idealism, for in addition to his senses and imagination he has mind; and mind, precisely because it is a thinking being, is an immaterial, pure being. How would it have been possible for one to conceive an immaterial being without an immaterial faculty and consequently without having immaterial conceptions? But man's mind is not so completely pure, in its absoluteness or in its range, as the mind or being of God. Man, or, rather, this man Leibniz, is thus a partial or semi-idealist, and only God is a complete idealist, "the perfect sage" (*der volkommene Weltweise*), as he is expressly called by Wolf. That means that God is the idea of the perfect, elaborate, absolute idealism of later speculative philosophy. For what is the mind or, generally, the being of God? It is nothing other than the mind and being of man separated from the determinations—be they real or assumed—that at certain times are bounds on man. He who does not have a mind that is torn asunder from the senses and who does not view the senses as bounds also does not view a mind without the senses as the highest and true intellect. What is, however, the idea of a thing if not its essence purified of the limitation and obscurity that it suffers in reality where it is related to other things? Thus, according to Leibniz, the limitation of the human mind lies in the fact that it is fixed to materialism, that is, obscure conceptions; these obscure conceptions arise only because the human being is related to other beings and to the world in general. But this relationship does not belong to the essence of the mind; rather, it contradicts the mind, for the mind in itself, that is, in the idea, is an immaterial being, that is, a being existing for itself and isolated. And this idea, or this mind, that is purified of all materialistic conceptions is precisely the divine mind. What was, however, merely an idea with Leibniz became truth and reality in later philosophy. Absolute idealism is nothing but the realized divine mind of Leibnizian theism; it is the pure mind systematically elaborated, which divests all things of their sensuousness, transforming them into pure entities of the mind, into thought-objects; it is the pure mind unattached to any foreign features, concerned only with itself as the essence of essences.

11

God is a thinking being; but the objects that he thinks and comprehends are, like his mind, not distinguished from his being. Thus, in thinking the objects, he thinks only himself, namely, he remains in an unbroken unity with himself. This unity of thought and the objects of thought is, however, the secret of speculative thought.

So, for example, in Hegel's *Logic* the objects of thought are not distinguished from the essence of thought. Thought stays here in an unbroken unity with itself! Its objects are only determinations of thought. They dissolve completely into it and keep for themselves nothing that would have remained outside the thought process. But that which is the essence of logic is also the essence of God. God is a spiritual, abstracted being; at the same time, however, he is the essence of being that embraces all beings in itself in unity with his abstracted being. But what are these beings that are identical to an abstracted, spiritual being? They themselves are abstracted beings—ideas. Things when existing in God are not the same as when they exist apart from him; they differ from real things to the same extent that things that are objects of logic differ from things that are the objects of real perception. To what, then, is the difference between divine and metaphysical thought reduced? Just to a difference of imagination, to a difference between thought that is merely imagined and real thought.

12

The difference between God's knowledge or thought, which as an archetype precedes the objects and creates them, and man's knowledge, which follows the objects as their copy, is nothing but the difference between a priori, or speculative, knowledge and a posteriori, or empirical, knowledge. Although theism conceives God as a thinking or a spiritual

being, at the same time it conceives him as a sensuous being. It
directly links, therefore, sensuous and material effects with the
thinking and willing of God. These effects contradict the essence of thought and will and express nothing more than the
power of nature. Such a material effect—consequently, a mere
expression of sensuous power—is above all the creation or the
bringing forth of the real and material world. Speculative
theology, on the other hand, transforms this sensuous act,
which contradicts the essence of thought, into a logical or
theoretical act, thus transforming the material creation of the
object into the speculative generation of the idea. In theism,
the world is a temporal product of God; the world has existed
for a few thousand years, and before it came into being there
was God. In speculative theology, on the other hand, the
world or nature is subsequent to God only according to rank
and significance; accident presupposes substance and nature
presupposes logic. This is according to the idea, but not according to sensuous existence and consequently not according
to time.

Theism, however, attributes to God not only speculative
but also—and indeed in its highest perfection—sensuous and
empirical knowledge. By the same token that the preworldly
and preobjective knowledge of God found its realization,
truth, and reality in the a priori knowledge of speculative
philosophy, so did the sensuous knowledge of God find its
realization, truth, and reality in the empirical sciences of the
modern era. The most perfect, and hence divine, sensuous
knowledge is indeed nothing other than the most sensuous
knowledge that knows the most minute objects and the least
noticeable details, that knows the hair on man's head not by
grasping it indiscriminately in one lock but by counting them,
thus knowing them all, hair by hair. "God is therefore the
all-knowing," says St. Thomas Aquinas, "because he knows the
most particular things." But this divine knowledge, which is
only an imaginary conception and a fantasy in theology, became rational and real knowledge in the knowledge of the
natural sciences gained through the telescope and microscope.

It counted the stars in the sky, the ova in the spawn of fish and butterflies, and the color spots on the wings of insects in order to distinguish them from one another; it alone demonstrated anatomically in the grub of the butterfly 288 muscles in the head, 1,647 in the body, and 2,186 in the stomach and intestines. What more can one ask? We have here an apparent example of the truth that man's conception of God is the human individual's conception of his own species, that God as the total of all realities or perfections is nothing other than the total of the attributes of the species—dispersed among men and realizing themselves in the course of world history—compendiously combined for the benefit of the limited individual. The domain of the natural sciences is, because of its quantitative size, completely beyond the capacity of the individual man to view and measure. Who is able to count the stars in the sky and at the same time the muscles and nerves in the body of the caterpillar? Lyonnet lost his sight over the anatomy of the caterpillar. Who is able to observe simultaneously the differences of height and depth on the moon and at the same time observe the differences of the innumerable ammonites and terebrates? But what the individual man does not know and cannot do all of mankind together knows and can do. Thus, the divine knowledge that knows simultaneously every particular has its reality in the knowledge of the species.

Not only divine omniscience but also divine omnipresence has realized itself in man. While one man notices what is happening on the moon or Uranus, another observes Venus or the intestines of the caterpillar or some other place that no human eye—while it was under the lordship of an omniscient and omnipresent God—has ever seen before. Indeed, while one man observes this star from the position of Europe, another observes the same star from the position of America. What is absolutely impossible for one man alone to accomplish is possible for two men to achieve. But God is in all places and knows all at the same time without distinction. Granted; but one should note that this omniscience and omnipresence exist only in the imagination and in fancy, and which, however, is human action. This is also valid regarding the predicate of this paragraph. Philosophy presupposes nothing; this is nothing more than to say that it abstracts from all objects given immediately, that is, objects given in sensation and thus distinguished from objects given in thought. In short, it abstracts from everything from which it is possible to abstract without stopping to think, and makes this act of abstracting from all objectivity the beginning of itself. What is, however, the absolute being if not the being for which nothing is to be presupposed and to which no object apart from itself is given and is necessary? What is it if not the being removed from all objects, from all sensuous things distinct and distinguishable from itself? What is it if not the being that, therefore, also becomes an object for man only through an abstraction from all these things? That from which God is free, from that you must liberate yourself if you want to reach God; and you make yourself really free when you conceive him. Consequently, if you think of God as a being that does not presuppose any other beings or objects, then you yourself will also think without presupposing an external object; the attribute that you affix to God is an attribute of your thought. Only what is activity in man is being in God or imagined as such. What, then, is the ego of Fichte that says, "I simply am because I am," or the pure, presuppositionless thought of Hegel if not the divine being of the old theology and metaphysics transformed into the present, active, and thinking being of man?

14

Speculative philosophy as the realization of God is at the same time the positing and the cancellation or negation of God, at the same time theism and atheism; for God, in the theological sense, is God only as long as he is conceived as a being distinguished from and independent of the being of man and nature. Theism that as the positing of God is at the same time the negation of God—or conversely as the negation of God is at the same time still the affirmation of God—is pantheism. Actual or theological theism is, however, nothing other than imaginary pantheism; imaginary pantheism is nothing other than real, true theism.

That which separates theism from pantheism is only the conception or the imagining of God as a personal being. All the determinations of God—and God is necessarily determined, otherwise he is nothing, not even an object of the imagination—are determinations of reality—of nature, of man, or of both. Hence, they are pantheistic determinations, for that which does not distinguish God from the being of nature or of man is pantheism. God is thus distinguished from the world, from the totality of nature and mankind, only by his personality or existence, but not by his determinations or his essence; that is, he is only imagined as a different being, but in truth he is not a different being. Theism is the contradiction of appearance and essence, imagination and truth, whereas pantheism is the unity of both; pantheism is the naked truth of theism. All the conceptions of theism, when grasped, seriously considered, carried out, and realized, lead necessarily to pantheism. Pantheism is consistent theism. Theism thinks of God as the cause—and indeed as a living and personal cause—and the creator of the world; God has brought forth the world by his will. But the will does not suffice. Where there is once will, there must also be mind; that which one wills is a matter of the mind. Without mind, there is no object. The things that God created existed, therefore, before their creation in God as objects of his mind, as entities of the mind. The mind of God is, it is said in theology, the total of all things and essences. Where else would they have sprung from, if not from nothingness? And it is irrelevant whether you conceive this nothingness in your imagination as independent or place it in God. But God contains, or is, everything only in an ideal manner, in the manner of the imagination. This ideal pantheism, however, leads necessarily to the real or the actual; for it is not far from God's mind to his being nor from his being to his reality. How could the mind allow itself to be separated from

the being, and how could the being allow itself to be separated from the reality or existence of God? If the objects are in
God's mind, how could they be apart from his being? If they
are the outcome of his mind, why not the outcome of his
being? If in God his being is directly identical with his reality and if God's existence is inseparable from the concept of
God, how could the conception of the object and the real object be separated in God's conception of things? How, then,
could the difference between the object in the conception and
the object apart from the conception, which constitutes only
the nature of the finite and nondivine mind, take place in God?
But, once we have no more objects apart from God's mind, so
we soon will also have no more objects apart from his being
and finally apart from his existence. All objects are in God,
and indeed in truth and actuality, not only in the imagination; for, when the objects are only in the imagination—of God
as well as of man—namely, when they are merely ideal or rather
imaginary in God, then they exist at the same time outside the
imagination, outside God. But, if we were once to have no
more objects and no world apart from God, so would we also
have no more God—not only an ideal and imagined, but a
real, being—apart from the world. In a word, we have Spinoz-
ism or pantheism.

Theism conceives God as a purely immaterial being. To
determine God as immaterial, however, means nothing else
than to determine matter as a thing of nothingness, as a nonbeing, for only God is the measure of reality. Only God is
being, truth, and essence; only what is valid in and through
God has being; what is denied of God has no being. To derive
matter from God means, therefore, nothing other than the
wish to prove the being of matter by its nonbeing, for deriva-
tion is the indication of a ground and a justification. God
made matter. But how, why, and from what? To this, theism
gives no answer. Matter for theism is a purely inexplicable
existence; that is, it is the limit, the end of theology on which
it is wrecked in life as well as in thought. How can I, then, derive the end and negation of theology from theology without

negating it? How can I look for explanation and information when theology's intelligence fails? How can I, from the negation of matter or the world, which is the essence of theology, from the proposition "matter does not exist," deduce—and, indeed, despite the God of theology—the affirmation of matter, the proposition "matter exists"? How else, but with mere fictions. Material things can only be derived from God, if God himself is determined as a material being. Only so will God change from an imagined and fancied cause into the real cause of the world. He who is not ashamed to make shoes should also not be ashamed to be and be called a shoemaker. Hans Sachs was, indeed, a shoemaker as well as a poet. But the shoes were the work of his hands, whereas his poems were the work of his mind. As the effect is, so is the cause. But matter is not God; it is, rather, the finite, the nondivine, the negation of God. The absolute admirers and followers of matter are atheists. Pantheism connects, therefore, atheism with theism, the negation of God with God; God is a material or, in the language of Spinoza, an extended being.

15

Pantheism is theological atheism or theological materialism. It is but the negation of theology on the grounds of theology, for it makes matter, which is the negation of God, into a predicate or attribute of the divine being. However, he who makes matter into an attribute of God declares matter to be a divine being. The realization of God presupposes in general the divinity, that is, the truth and essentiality, of the real. The divinization of the real, of that which exists materially— materialism, empiricism, realism, humanism—and the negation of theology are, however, the essence of the modern era. Pantheism is, therefore, nothing other than the essence of the modern era elevated to a divine being and to a religiophilosophical principle.

Empiricism or realism—by which is here understood generally the so-called real sciences, especially the natural sciences—

negates theology. It is, however, not a theoretical but a practical negation; it is a negation by means of the act through which the realist makes that which is the negation of God, or at least is not God, into the essential business of his life and the essential object of his activity. He, however, who concentrates with heart and mind on the material and sensuous only, actually denies the supernatural its reality; for only that is real, at least for man, that is an object of true and real activity. "What I don't know doesn't hurt me." The statement that one cannot know anything of the supernatural is only an excuse. God and divine things are no longer known only when one does not want to know them. How much was known of God, of the devils, or of the angels as long as these supernatural beings were still objects of a real faith! That in which one is interested is also the thing in which one is proficient. The mystics and scholastics of the Middle Ages had no ability and aptitude for natural science only because they had no interest in nature. Wherever the disposition is not lacking, there also the senses and organs are not lacking. That to which the heart is open is also accessible to the mind. Thus, mankind in the modern era lost the organs for the supernatural world and its secrets only because it lost together with the faith also the disposition toward the supernatural world, because its essential tendency was anti-Christian and antitheological; that is, it was an anthropological, cosmic, realistic, and materialistic tendency.[1] Spinoza hit the nail on the head, therefore, with his paradoxical proposition: God is an extended, that is, material being. He found, at least for his time, the true philosophic expression for the materialistic tendency of the modern era; he legitimized and sanctioned it: God himself is a materialist. Spinoza's philosophy was religion; he himself was a remarkable person. With him, materialism was not, as it was with so many others, in contradiction to the conception of an immaterial and antimaterialistic God who consequently also orders only antimaterialistic, heavenly tendencies and activities as

[1] The differences between materialism, empiricism, realism, and humanism are in this work irrelevant.

that is, nothing real; but it attributes this nonbeing not to the object, but only to itself, to its knowledge. The empiricist does not deny God's being, that is, maintaining God as a dead and indifferent being; but he denies God the being that proves itself as being, that is effective, palpable, and active in life. He affirms God, but negates all the consequences necessarily connected with this affirmation. He repudiates theology and gives it up; yet not for theoretical reasons, but rather because of aversion to, and dislike of the objects of theology, that is, because of an obscure feeling of their unreality. The empiricist thinks to himself that theology is nothing, but he also adds "for me"; that means that his judgment is subjective and pathological. For he does not have the freedom, but also not the desire and the vocation, to bring the objects of theology before the forum of reason. This is the vocation of philosophy. The task of modern philosophy was therefore nothing other than to elevate the pathological judgment of empiricism that there is nothing in theology to a theoretical and objective judgment, to transform the indirect, unconscious, and negative negation of theology into a direct, positive, and conscious negation. How ridiculous it is, therefore, to wish to suppress the "atheism" of philosophy without suppressing at the same time the atheism of experience! How ridiculous it is to persecute the theoretical negation of Christianity and at the same time to let the actual negations of Christianity, in which the modern era abounds, stand as they are! How ridiculous it is to believe that with the consciousness, that is, the symptom, of evil the cause of evil is simultaneously abolished! Indeed, how ridiculous! And yet how rich with such ridiculous things is history! They repeat themselves in all critical periods. No wonder! For, with regard to the past, all is looked on favorably, and the necessity of the changes and revolutions that occurred is acknowledged; its application, however, to the present situation is opposed with every means available. The present is made the exception to the rule because of shortsightedness and complacency.

17

The elevation of matter to a divine being is directly and simultaneously the elevation of reason to a divine being. That which the theist—because of emotional needs and the demand for unlimited bliss—denies God by means of the imagination is affirmed of God by the pantheist because of rational needs. Matter is an essential object of reason. If there were no matter, reason would have no stimulus and substance for thinking and thus no content. Matter cannot be given up without giving up reason; nor can it be acknowledged without acknowledging reason. Materialists are rationalists. Pantheism, however, affirms reason only indirectly as a divine being, namely, by transforming God from a being of imagination, which he is as a personal being in theism, into an object of reason and a being thereof. The direct apotheosis of reason is idealism. Pantheism leads necessarily to idealism. Idealism is related to pantheism in the same way as pantheism is related to theism.

As the object is, so is the subject. According to Descartes, the essence of corporeal things, the body as substance, is not an object of the senses, but only of the mind. But precisely therefore it is also, according to Descartes, not the senses but the mind that is the essence of the perceiving subject, that is, of man. Essence is given as an object only to essence. According to Plato, opinion has as object only impermanent things; therefore, however, it is itself impermanent and changing knowledge—indeed, only opinion. The essence of music is the highest essence to the musician, and, therefore, the ear is to him the highest organ; he would sooner lose his eyes than his ears. The natural scientist, on the other hand, would rather lose his ears than his eyes, because his objective being is light. If I make the tone divine, I also make the ear divine. If I speak like a pantheist, saying that God or, what amounts to the same, absolute being or absolute truth and reality is an object only for and of reason, then I explain God as a rational being or a being of reason and express thereby indirectly only the absolute truth and reality of reason. It is therefore necessary that reason return to itself, reverse this inverted self-recognition, and declare itself directly as the absolute truth, thus becoming directly, without the mediation of another object, its own object as absolute truth. The pantheist says the same thing as the idealist, except that he expresses himself objectively or realistically, whereas the idealist expresses himself subjectively or idealistically. The former has his idealism in the object: apart from substance, apart from God, there is nothing, and all things are only determinations of God. The latter has his pantheism in the ego: apart from the ego, there is nothing, and all things exist only as objects of the ego. But, nevertheless, idealism is the truth of pantheism; this is so because God or substance is only the object of reason, of the ego, and of the thinking being. If I believe or think generally of no God, then by the same token I have no God. He exists for me only through me, and he exists for reason only through reason. The a priori, or first, being is, thus, not the being that is thought, but the thinking being; not the object, but the subject. By the same token that natural science turned necessarily from the light back to the eye, so philosophy necessarily turned from the objects of thinking back to the subject of thinking, that is, the ego. What is light—as the being that brightens and illumines, as the object of optics—without the eye? It is nothing. And thus far goes natural science. But what, philosophy now further asks, is the eye without consciousness? It is also nothing. It is identical whether I see without consciousness or whether I do not see. Only the consciousness of seeing is the reality of seeing or real seeing. But why do you believe that something exists apart from you? Because you see, hear, and feel something. Thus, this something is a real something, a real object only as an object of consciousness; and consciousness is the absolute reality, the measure of all existence. All that exists, exists only as being for consciousness, as comprehended in consciousness; for consciousness is first and foremost being. Thus, the essence of theology realizes itself in idealism, and the essence of God, in the ego and in con-

sciousness. Without God, nothing can exist and nothing can be
thought. In terms of idealism, this means that everything
exists only as an object, be it a real or a possible object, of
consciousness. To exist means to be an object, thus presupposing consciousness. Things, the world in general, are
the work and product of an absolute being, of God;
but this absolute being is an ego, a conscious and thinking being. Thus, as Descartes, from the viewpoint of theism, so
well says, the world is an *Ens rationis divinae,* an idea, a
chimera of God. But this idea itself is again only a vague
conception in theism and theology. If we, therefore, realize
this conception, if we, so to speak, carry out practically what
in theism is only theory, then we have the world as a product
of the ego (Fichte) or—at least in its appearance and in our
intuition of it—as a work or product of our intuition and
understanding (Kant). "Nature is derived from the laws of
the possibility of experience in general." "The understanding
does not derive its laws (a priori) from nature, but rather it
prescribes them to it." Kantian idealism, in which the objects
conform to the understanding and not the understanding to
the objects, is therefore nothing other than the realization of
the theological conception of the divine mind, which is not
determined by the objects but rather determines them. How
silly it is, therefore, to acknowledge idealism in heaven, that is,
the idealism of the imagination, as a divine truth, but reject
idealism on earth, that is, the idealism of reason, as a human
error. Deny idealism and you also deny God! God only is the
creator of idealism. If you do not want the consequences, then
you also should not want the principle! Idealism is nothing
but rational or rationalized theism. But Kant's idealism is still
a limited idealism—idealism based on the viewpoint of empiricism. According to what has been said above, God is for empiricism still only a being in conception and in theory—in
the ordinary, bad sense—but not in actuality and truth, a
thing in itself, but no longer a thing for empiricism, because
only empirical and real objects are objects for empiricism.
Matter is the only material for its thinking; it has therefore

no more matter for God. God exists, but he is for us a *tabula rasa,* an empty being, a mere idea. God, as we conceive and think of him, is our ego, our mind, and our essence; but this God is only an appearance of us and for us, not God in himself. Kant's idealism is the idealism still bound by theism. We often find that, having been freed long ago in actuality from a matter, a doctrine, or an idea, we are at the same time not freed from it in the mind. It is no longer a truth in our existence—perhaps it was never that—but it is still a theoretical truth, a limit on our mind. Mind, because it takes things most thoroughly, is also the last to be free. Theoretical freedom is, at least in many things, the last freedom. How many are republicans in their heart and by their disposition, but in their minds, cannot detach themselves from the monarchy? Their republican hearts are wrecked by the objections and difficulties that the mind presents. So is it also with the theism of Kant. Kant has realized and negated theology in morality and the divine essence in the will. For Kant, the will is the true, original, and unconditional being originating in itself. In actuality, the predicates of the Godhead are claimed by Kant for the will; his theism still has, therefore, only the significance of a theoretical limit. Fichte is a Kant liberated from the limits of theism; he is "the messiah of speculative reason." Fichte's is Kantian idealism, but from the viewpoint of idealism. According to Fichte, the conception of a God who is distinct from us and exists apart from us is given only in the empirical viewpoint. But in truth, from the viewpoint of idealism, the thing in itself, God (since God is the real thing in itself), is only the ego in itself, that is, the ego that is distinct from the individual and empirical ego. Outside the ego, there is no God: "Our religion is reason." But Fichte's idealism is only the negation and realization of abstract and formal theism, of monotheism; it is not the negation and realization of religious and material theism, which is full of content, of trinitarianism, whose realization is "absolute," or Hegelian, idealism. One can put it this way: Fichte has realized the God of pantheism only insofar as he is a thinking being, but not insofar as he is an extended and material being. Fichte's is theistic idealism; Hegel's is pantheistic idealism.

18

Modern philosophy has realized and negated the divine being who is separated and distinguished from sensation, the world, and man. But it realized and negated this divine being only in thought, in reason, and indeed in that reason that is also separated and distinguished from sensation, the world, and man. Namely, modern philosophy has proved only the divinity of mind; it recognized only mind, and indeed the abstract mind, as the divine and absolute being. Descartes' definition of himself as mind, namely, "My essence consists only of the fact that I think," is modern philosophy's definition of itself. The will of Kantian and Fichtean idealism is itself a pure being of the mind; and perception—which Schelling, unlike Fichte, connected with the mind—is only fantasy, untruth, and does not come into consideration.

Modern philosophy proceeded from theology; it is indeed nothing other than theology dissolved and transformed into philosophy. The abstract and transcendental being of God could, therefore, be realized and negated only in an abstract and transcendent way. In order to transform God into reason, reason itself had to assume the quality of an abstract, divine being. The senses, says Descartes, give neither true reality, being, nor certainty; only mind separated from the senses gives truth. Whence this cleavage between the mind and the senses? It is derived only from theology. God is not a sensuous being; he is, rather, the negation of all sensuous determinations and is only known through the abstraction from sensation. But he is God, that is, the truest, the most real, and the most certain being. Whence should truth come to the senses, which are born atheists? God is the being in which existence cannot be separated from essence and concept and which cannot be thought except as existing. Descartes transforms this objective being into a subjective one and the ontological proof into a psychological one; he transforms the proposition, "because God is thinkable, therefore he exists," into the proposition, "I think, therefore I am." As in God there is no separation of being from being thought, so in me—as mind, which is however my essence—being cannot be separated from thought; and, as in the former, so also here this inseparableness constitutes the essence. A being that exists—regardless whether in itself or for me—only as a being of thought, as an object of abstraction from all sensation, necessarily also realizes and subjectifies itself only in a being that exists solely as thought and whose essence is solely abstract thought.

19

The culmination of modern philosophy is the Hegelian philosophy. The historical necessity and justification of modern philosophy attaches itself, therefore, mainly to the critique of Hegel.

20

The new philosophy has, according to its historical origin, the same task and position toward modern philosophy that the latter had toward theology. The new philosophy is the realization of the Hegelian philosophy or, generally, of the philosophy that prevailed until now, a realization, however, which is at the same time the negation, and indeed the negation without contradiction, of this philosophy.

21

The contradiction of modern philosophy, especially of pantheism, is due to the fact that it is the negation of theology from the viewpoint of theology or the negation of theology that itself is again theology; this contradiction characterizes especially the Hegelian philosophy.

The immaterial being as a pure object of the mind, as a pure entity of the mind, is for modern philosophy and also for Hegelian philosophy the only true and absolute being, that is, God. Even matter, which Spinoza made into an attribute of the divine substance, is a metaphysical object, a pure entity of the mind, for the essential determination of matter as distinguished from the mind, from the activity of thinking—namely, the determination making it a passive being—is taken away here. But Hegel differs from earlier philosophy in that he determines differently the relationship between material, sensuous beings and immaterial beings. The former philosophers and theologians thought of the true, divine being as a being that in itself, by nature, is detached and liberated from sensation and matter. They placed the effort and labor of abstraction and of self-liberation from the sensuous only in themselves, in order to reach that which in itself is already free from the sensuous. To this freedom, they attributed the divine bliss and, to this self-liberation, the virtue of the human being. Hegel, on the other hand, transforms this subjective activity into the self-activity of the divine being. God himself must undertake this labor and, like the heroes of paganism, fight through virtue for his divinity. Only in this way does the liberation of the absolute from matter—which otherwise is only an assumption and a conception—become actuality and truth. But this self-liberation from matter can be attributed to God only if at the same time matter is attributed to him. But how can matter be attributed to God? Only in that he himself attributes it. But in God there is only God. Then, only in that he posits himself as matter, as non-God, that is, as his otherness. Thus, matter is not a preceding opposite of the ego and of spirit, in a way which would be inconceivable; it is the self-alienation of spirit. Thus, matter itself receives spirit and mind; it is taken up into the absolute being as a moment in its life, growth, and development. However, at the same time, matter is nevertheless posited again as an invalid and untrue being in that only the being that restores itself out of this alienation, that is, that detaches itself from sensation and from

matter expresses itself as the completed being in its true structure and form. The natural, material, and sensuous—and, indeed, the sensuous, not in the moral and ordinary sense, but
in the metaphysical—are to be negated here, as nature which
is poisoned by original sin is negated in theology. It is indeed
assimilated into reason, the ego, and the spirit; but it is the
irrational element in reason, the nonego in the ego—the negative in them. For example, in Schelling, nature in God is the
nondivine in God which being in him is apart from him,
and, for example, in Cartesian philosophy, the body, although
connected with me, that is, with the spirit, is nevertheless
apart from me, not belonging to me, that is, to my essence; it
is, therefore, irrelevant whether it is connected with me. Matter continues to contradict the being that philosophy presupposes as the true being.

Matter is indeed posited in God, that is, it is posited as God,
and 'to posit matter as God amounts to saying "There is no
God," or, what amounts to the same, it is to renounce theology
and to recognize the truth of materialism. But at the same
time the truth of the essence of theology is nevertheless presupposed. Atheism, the negation of theology, is therefore negated again; that is, theology is restored through philosophy.
God is God only because he overcomes and negates matter,
that is, the negation of God. And, according to Hegel, only the
negation of the negation is the true affirmation. In the end, we
are again at the point from which we started—in the bosom of
Christian theology. Thus, we already have in the main principle of Hegel's philosophy the principle and outcome of his
philosophy of religion, namely, that philosophy does not negate the dogmas of theology, but only restores and mediates
them through the negation of rationalism. The secret of the
Hegelian dialectic lies, in the last analysis, only in the fact
that it negates theology by philosophy and then, in turn,
negates philosophy by theology. Theology constitutes the beginning and the end; philosophy stands in the middle as the
negation of the first affirmation, but the negation of the negation is theology. At first everything is overthrown, but then

everything is put again in its former place; it is the same as with Descartes. The Hegelian philosophy is the last magnificent attempt to restore Christianity, which was lost and wrecked, through philosophy and, indeed, to restore Christianity—as is generally done in the modern era—by identifying it with the negation of Christianity. The much-praised speculative identity of mind and matter, of the infinite and the finite, and of the divine and the human is nothing more than the unfortunate contradiction of the modern era. It is the identity of faith and disbelief, theology and philosophy, religion and atheism, Christianity and paganism, placed on its highest summit, on the summit of metaphysics. This contradiction is placed out of sight and obscured in Hegel only because the negation of God, that is, atheism, is made into an objective determination of God; God is determined as a process, and atheism is determined as a moment in this process. But, by the same token that a faith that is restored from disbelief is hardly a true faith—because it is always a faith attached to its contradiction—so is the God who is restored from his own negation hardly a true God; he is rather a self-contradictory, atheistic God.

22

Just as the divine essence is nothing other than the essence of man liberated from the limits of nature, so is the essence of absolute idealism nothing other than the essence of subjective idealism liberated from the limits, and, indeed, rational limits, of subjectivity, that is, from sensation or objectivity in general. The Hegelian philosophy can therefore be directly derived from Kantian and Fichtean idealism.

Kant says:

When we consider—as, indeed, we ought to—the objects of the senses as mere appearances, so we admit at the same time, by doing so, that they are based on a thing in itself, although we may not know how it is constituted in itself, but only its appearance, that is, the way in which our senses are affected by this unknown something. Thus the understanding, just because it accepts appearances, admits also the existence of things in themselves, and thus we can say that the conception of such beings—which lie at the basis of appearances and are, consequently, mere objects of the mind—is not only possible, but unavoidable.

The objects of the senses, of experience, are thus for the mind mere appearance and not the truth; they do not satisfy the mind, that is, they do not correspond to its essence. The mind is consequently in no way limited in its essence by the senses; otherwise, it would not take the sensuous objects for appearances, but for the straight truth. That which does not satisfy me does not restrict and limit me either. And still the entities of the mind should not be real objects for the mind! Kant's philosophy is the contradiction of subject and object, essence and existence, thought and being. Essence lies here in the mind, whereas existence lies in the senses. Existence without essence is mere appearance—these are the sensuous objects; essence without existence is mere idea—these are the entities of the mind, the noumena. They are thought, but they lack objectivity and existence, at least existence for us. They are the things in themselves, the true things, but they are not real things, and consequently they are also not objects for the mind, that is, they cannot be determined and known by the mind. But what a contradiction to separate the truth from reality and reality from the truth! If we negate this contradiction, we have the philosophy of identity, where the objects of the mind and the things that are thought exist as the true and also as the real things, where the essence and constitution of the objects of the mind correspond to the essence and constitution of the mind or of the subject, and where the subject is no longer limited and conditioned by a substance existing apart from it and contradicting its essence. But the subject, which has no longer an object apart from itself and consequently is no longer limited, is no longer a "finite" subject—no longer the "I" opposite whom an object stands; it is the absolute being whose theological or popular expression is the word "God." It is indeed the same subject and the same "I" as in

Thus spoke Schelling, and it is the same with Hegel. The essence of Hegelian logic is thought deprived of its determinateness in which it thinks, i.e., in which lies the activity of subjectivity. The third part of the *Logic* is, and is indeed explicitly called, the subjective logic; and yet the forms of subjectivity that are the object of that part are not to be subjective. The concept, the judgment, the conclusion—indeed, even such particular forms of conclusion and judgment as the problematic or assertoric judgment—are not our concepts, judgments, and conclusions; no, they are objective, absolute forms existing in and for themselves. So does absolute philosophy externalize and alienate from man his own essence and activity! Hence the violence and torture that it inflicts on our minds. We ought not to think of that which is ours as our own; we ought to abstract from the determination by which something is what it is, namely, we ought to think of it without sense and take it in the non-sense of the absolute. Nonsense is the highest essence of theology—of ordinary as well as of speculative theology.

What Hegel disapprovingly observes regarding Fichte's philosophy—namely, that everyone believes the ego to be in himself, that everyone is reminded of himself and yet does not find the ego in himself—is valid for speculative philosophy in general. It comprehends almost all things in a sense by which they are no longer recognized. And the cause of this evil is indeed theology. The divine and absolute being must distinguish itself from finite, that is, real, beings. But we have no determinations for the absolute except the determinations of real things, be they natural or human things. How do these determinations become determinations of the absolute? Only in that they are taken in a sense that differs from their real meaning, that is, in an entirely reversed sense. Everything that exists in finiteness exists also in the absolute; but it exists differently in the absolute. Totally different laws are valid there; that which is for us pure nonsense is reason and wisdom there. Speculation uses the name of a thing without accepting the notion that is linked with it; hence, the boundless arbitrariness of speculation. Speculation excuses its arbitrariness by saying that it chooses for its notions names from the language, to which, however, "ordinary consciousness" attaches concepts that have only a far-fetched similarity to these notions; so now it is the fault of the language. But the fault lies in the matter, in the principle of speculation itself. The contradiction in speculation between name and object, conception and notion, is nothing other than the old theological contradiction between the determinations of the divine being, taken only in a symbolical or analogical sense, and the determinations of the human being, taken in an essential and real sense. At any rate, philosophy need not care about the conceptions that common usage or misuse attaches to a name; philosophy, however, has to bind itself to the determined nature of things, whose signs are names.

24

The identity of thought and being that is the central point of the philosophy of identity is nothing other than the necessary consequence and elaboration of the notion of God as the being whose notion or essence contains existence. Speculative philosophy has only generalized and made into an attribute of thought or of the notion in general what theology made into an exclusive attribute of the notion of God. The identity of thought and being is therefore only the expression of the divinity of reason—that thought or reason is the absolute being, the total of all truth and reality, that there is nothing in contrast to reason, rather that reason is everything just as God is, in strict theology, everything, that is, all essential and true being. But a being that is not distinguished from thought and that is only a predicate or a determination of reason is only an ideated and abstracted being; but in truth it is not being. The identity of thought and being expresses, therefore, only the identity of thought with itself; that means that absolute thought never extricates itself from itself to become being. Being remains in another world. Absolute philosophy has indeed transformed for us the other world of theology into this world, but in turn it has transformed for us this side of the real world into the other world.

The thought of speculative or absolute philosophy—in distinction from itself as the activity of mediation—determines being as immediate and unmediated. For thought—at least for that thought that we have here before us—being is nothing more than this. Thought places being in opposition to itself, but within itself, and thus it invalidates directly and without difficulty the opposition of being vis-à-vis itself; for being, as the opposition of thought within thought, is nothing other than an idea itself. If being is nothing more than being unmediated, if nonmediation alone constitutes its distinction from thought, how easy it is, then, to prove that the determination of nonmediation, namely, being, belongs also to thought! If a mere determination of ideas constitutes the essence of being, how should being be distinguished from thought?

25

The proof that something is has no other meaning than that something is not only thought of. This proof cannot, however, be derived from thought itself. If being is to be added to an object of thought, so must something distinct from thought be added to thought itself.

The example of the difference between a hundred dollars in conception and a hundred dollars in reality—which was chosen by Kant in the critique of the ontological proof to designate the difference between thought and being and which was, however, mocked by Hegel—is essentially quite true. For I have the hundred dollars only in the mind, but the other dollars I have in the hand. The former exist just for me; the latter, however, exist also for others—they can be felt and seen. But only that exists that is at the same time for me and others, on which I and others agree—what is not only mine but is general.

In thought as such, I find myself being in identity with myself; here I am absolute master, and nothing contradicts me; here I am judge and litigant at the same time; here there is consequently no critical difference between the object and my ideas of it. But, if it simply concerns the being of an object, then I cannot consult myself only, but must take the evidence of witnesses who are apart from me. These witnesses that are distinguished from me as thought are the senses. Being is something in which not only I but also others, above all also the object itself, participate. Being means being a subject, being for itself. And it is truly not the same whether I am a subject or only an object, whether I am a being for myself or only a being for another being, that is, only an idea. Where I am a mere object of conception, where I consequently am no longer myself, where I am like a man after death, there I must put up with everything; there it is possible for another person to portray me in a way that would be a true caricature without my being able to protest against it. But, when I am still really existing, then I can thwart him, then I can make him feel and prove to him that there is a vast difference between me as I am in his conception and me as I am in reality, namely, between me as his object and me as a subject. In thought, I am an absolute subject; I accept everything only as my object or predicate, that is, as object or predicate of a thinking self; I am intolerant. In the activity of the senses, on the other hand, I am liberal; I let the object be what I myself am—a subject, a real and self-actualizing being. Only sense and perception give me something as subject.

26

A being that only thinks, and thinks abstractly, has no conception at all of being, of existence, or of reality. Being is the boundary of thought; being as being is not an object of philosophy, at least not of abstract and absolute philosophy. Speculative philosophy itself expresses this indirectly in that for it being is equal to nonbeing—nothing is. Nothing, however, is not an object of thought.

Being as the object of speculative thought is simply the unmediated, that is, the undetermined, object; thus, there is nothing to think about or distinguish in being. But speculative thought is for itself the measure of all reality; it declares only this, in which it finds activity for itself and which provides it with substance for thought, to be something. For abstract thought, being is therefore nothing in itself and for itself, because it is the nothingness of thought, that is, it is nothing for thought—it is the thoughtless. Precisely because of this, this being is also—as it is drawn by speculative philosophy into its domain and claimed as its notion—a pure ghost, standing in absolute contradiction to real being and to that which man understands by being. Namely, by being man understands an existence according to objects and reason, which is being-for-itself, reality, existence, actuality, and objectivity. All these determinations or names express one and the same thing, only from different points of view. Being in thought, without objectivity, reality, or being-for-itself is, of course, nothing; but in this nothingness I only announce the nothingness of my abstraction.

27

"Being" in the Hegelian logic is the "being" of the old metaphysics that is attributed without differentiation to all objects because, according to the old metaphysics, all things agree in that they are. This uniform being is, however, an abstract idea without reality. Being is as varied as the objects that exist.

It is maintained, for example, in a metaphysical theory of Wolf's school, that God, the world, man, the table, the book, and so forth agree with one another in that they are. And Christian Thomasius says: "Being is everywhere the same. Essence is as manifold as the objects." This being that is everywhere the same, without difference and without content, is also the being of the Hegelian logic. Hegel himself observes that the polemic against the identity of being and nothingness derives only from the fact that being is given a definite content. But the consciousness of being is indeed always and necessarily bound to a definite content. If I abstract from the content of being and indeed from every content, since everything is the content of being, then I am left, to be sure, with nothing more than the idea of nothingness. And when, therefore, Hegel reproaches common consciousness for having substituted for being as an object of logic something that does not belong to being, so can he be much more readily reproached for having substituted a groundless abstraction for what man's consciousness rightly and rationally understands as being. Being is not a general notion that can be separated from objects. It is one with that which exists. It is thinkable only through mediation; it is thinkable only through the predicates on which the essence of an object is based. Being is the positing of essence. That which is my essence is my being. The fish exists in water; you cannot, however, separate its essence from this being. Language already identifies being and essence. Only in human life, however, indeed only in abnormal and unfortunate cases, is being separated from essence; only here does it happen that a person's essence is not where his being is. But also precisely because of this separation a person is not truly with his soul where he is really with his body. You are there only where your heart is. All beings, except in cases contrary to nature, like to be where and what they are; that is, their essence is not separated from their being, and their being is not separated from their essence. And consequently you cannot posit being as simply identical with itself in distinction from the variety of essence. Being after its removal from all the essential qualities of the objects is only your conception of being—a being that is made up and invented, without the essence of being.

28

The Hegelian philosophy did not overcome the contradiction of thought and being. That being with which the *Phe-*

nomenology starts stands in the most direct contradiction to real being no less than that being with which the *Logic* starts.

This contradiction becomes apparent in the *Phenomenology* in the form of the *Dies* ["this"] and the *Allgemeinen* ["the general"]; for the particular belongs to being, and the general belongs to thought. In the *Phenomenology*, however, the former and the latter flow together, indistinguishable for thought; but what an immense difference there is between the "this" as an object of abstract thought and the "this" as an object of reality! This wife, for example, is my wife, and this house is my house, although everyone speaks, as I do, of his house and his wife as "this house" and "this wife." The indifference and uniformity of the logical "this" is here interrupted and destroyed by the legal meaning of the word. Were we to accept the logical "this" in natural law, we would directly arrive at a community of goods and wives where there is no difference between this and that and where everyone possesses every woman; we would arrive at the negation of all rights, for rights are founded only on the reality of the difference between this and that.

We have before us in the beginning of the *Phenomenology* nothing other than the contradiction between the word, which is general, and the object, which is always a particular. And the idea that relies only on the word will not overcome this contradiction. Just as the word is not the object, so is the being that is spoken or ideated not real being. Were one to reply that Hegel deals with being, not from the practical viewpoint, as here, but from the theoretical viewpoint, I would be obliged to reciprocate by saying that the practical viewpoint is here completely justified. The question of being is indeed a practical question in which our being participates; it is a question of life and death. And, when we hold fast to our being in the law, so also we do not want logic to take it away from us. It must be recognized by logic also, unless it wants to persevere in its contradiction with real being. By the way, the practical viewpoint—the viewpoint of eating and drinking—is itself taken by the *Phenomenology* in order to refute the truth of sensuous, that is, particular being. But here, also, I owe my existence never to the linguistic or logical bread—bread in itself —but always only to *this* bread, to the "unutterable! " Being that is founded on many such unutterable things is therefore itself something unutterable. It is indeed the ineffable. Where words cease, life first begins, and the secret of being is first disclosed. If, therefore, being unutterable is being irrational, then the whole of existence is irrational because it is always and forever only *this* existence. But it is not irrational. Existence has meaning and rationality for itself, also without being utterable.

29

Thought that "overleaps its otherness"—the "otherness of thought" is, however, being—is thought that oversteps its natural boundaries. Thought overleaps its opposite; this means that thought claims for itself what belongs not to itself but to being. Particularity and individuality, however, belong to being, whereas generality belongs to thought. Thought thus claims for itself particularity; it makes the negation of generality (namely, particularity that is the essential form of sensation) into a moment in thought. So does "abstract" thought or the abstract notion, which has being apart from itself, become a "concrete" notion.

But how does man arrive at this point where thought trespasses into the domain of being? He reaches this point through theology. In God, being is directly bound to the essence or the notion, the form of existence with the generality of the particular. The "concrete notion" is God transformed into the notion. But how does man reach "concrete" or absolute thought from "abstract" thought? How does he arrive at theology from philosophy? The answer to this question was already given by history itself in the transition from ancient pagan philosophy to the so-called neo-Platonic philosophy, for neo-Platonic philosophy differentiates itself from ancient philosophy only in that it is theology, whereas ancient pagan philosophy is only philosophy. Ancient philosophy had reason, the "idea," for its principle; but "the idea was not posited by Plato and Aristotle as the all-comprehending." Ancient philosophy left something existing apart from thought; it left a residue that was not absorbed in thought. The image of this being apart from thought is matter—the substratum of reality. Reason found its boundary in matter. Ancient philosophy still lived in the distinction between thought and being; thought, the mind or the idea, was for it still not the all-comprehending, that is, the unique, exclusive, and absolute reality. The ancient philosophers were still wise men, that is, physiologists, politicians, zoologists; in short, they were anthropologists, not theologians, or at least only partly theologians. To be sure, precisely for this reason they were also at first only partially anthropologists, hence limited and defective anthropologists. To the neo-Platonic philosophers, on the other hand, matter— namely, the material and real world in general—is no longer an authority and a reality. Fatherland, family, worldly ties, and goods in general, which the ancient peripatetic philosophy still counted as man's bliss—all these are nothing for the neo-Platonic sage. He even considers death better than corporeal life; he does not include the body in his essence; he transfers bliss to the soul only and separates himself from all corporeal, in short, external things. When, however, man has nothing else apart from himself, he searches and finds everything in himself; he posits in place of the real world the imaginary and intelligible world in which there is everything that is in the real world, but abstracted and imagined. Even matter can be found in the immaterial world of the neo-Platonists, but it is here only ideated and imagined matter. And, where man has no longer a being apart from himself, he posits a being in his thought, which, though it is a being of thought, still has the properties of a real being, which as an unsensuous being is at the same time a sensuous being and which as a theoretical object is at the same time a practical object. This being is God—the highest good of the neo-Platonists. Man satisfies himself only in essence. He therefore substitutes for himself an ideal being in place of the real being, that is, he now attributes to his conceptions and ideas the essence of the reality that he had relinquished or lost. The imagination is no longer an imagination for him, but the object itself; the image is no longer an image, but the thing itself; thought and idea—reality. Precisely because he no longer relates himself as a subject to a real world as his object, his conceptions become for him objects, beings, spirits, and gods. The more abstract he is, the more negative he is toward the real and the sensuous and the more sensuous he is precisely in abstraction. God, the One—who is the highest object and being of abstraction, thus abstracted from all manifold and differences, that is, sensation —is known by contact and direct presence ($\Pi\alpha\rho o \upsilon\sigma\acute{\iota}\alpha$). Indeed, as the lowest thing, matter, so also the highest thing, the One, is known through nonknowledge and ignorance. That means that the merely ideated, abstracted, nonsensuous, and supersensuous being is at the same time a really existing, sensuous being.

Just as when a man commits suicide he negates the body, this rational limit of subjectivity, so when he lapses into fantastic and transcendental practice he associates himself with embodied divine and ghostly appearances, namely, he negates in practice the difference between imagination and perception. Thus also is lost theoretically the difference between thought and being, subjective and objective, sensuous and nonsensuous, where matter is for him not a reality and consequently is not a boundary of thinking reason and where for him reason, that is, the intellectual being and the being of subjectivity in general, is in its limitlessness the sole and absolute being. Thought negates everything, but only in order to posit everything in itself. It has no longer a boundary in something apart from itself; therefore, it itself steps out of its immanent and natural boundary. So does reason, the idea, become concrete; namely, that which perception should give is appropriated by thought, and that which is the function and concern of the senses, of perception and of life, becomes the function and concern of thought. So is the concrete made into a predicate of thought and being into a mere determination of thought; for the proposition "the notion is concrete" is identical with the proposition "being is a determination of thought." That which is imagination and fantasy with the neo-Platonists was merely rationalized and transformed by Hegel into concepts. Hegel is not "the German or Christian Aristotle"; he is the German Proclus. Absolute philosophy is the reborn Alexandrian philosophy. According to Hegel's explicit determination, it is not the Aristotelian nor generally ancient pagan philosophy that is the absolute philosophy. It is Alexandrian philosophy that is the Christian philosophy (although to be sure still mixed with pagan ingredients) and the absolute philosophy (although still at the elementary stage of abstracting from concrete self-consciousness).

Let it be further noted that neo-Platonic theology shows with particular clarity that, as the object is, so is the subject, and vice versa; consequently, the object of theology is nothing other than the objectified essence of the subject, that is, of man. For the neo-Platonist, God in the highest degree is the simple, the singular, the simply undetermined and indistinct. He is not a being, but rather above being, for being is still determined by the fact that it is a being. He is not a notion or mind, but rather without and above mind, for mind, too, is determined by the fact that it is mind; and, where there is mind, there also is distinction and separation into thinking and being thought, which consequently cannot occur in the plainly simple. But what is objectively the highest being for the neo-Platonist is also the highest being subjectively; that which he posits in the object, in God, as being he posits in himself as activity and striving. To have no longer any distinction, to have no mind or self, is and means being God. But that which God is the neo-Platonist strives to become; the goal of his activity is to cease "being a self, mind, and reason." Ecstasy or rapture is for the neo-Platonist the highest psychological state of man. This state objectified as being is the divine being. Thus, God is derived only from man, but not conversely, at least originally, man from God. This is shown with particular clarity also in the neo-Platonists' determination of God as the self-sufficient and blissful being, for where else than in the pains and needs of man does this being who is without pain and without needs have its ground and origin? With the lack of need and pain, the imagination and feeling of bliss also collapse. Only in contrast to misery is bliss a reality. Only in man's wretchedness does God have his birthplace. Only from man does God derive all his determinations. God is what man would like to be; he is man's own essence and goal conceived as a real being. Here also lies the distinctiveness of the neo-Platonist as compared to the Stoic, Epicurean, and Skeptic. Absence of passion, bliss, self-sufficiency, freedom, and independence were also the goals of these philosophers, but only as virtues of man; that means that their ground was still the concrete and real man as truth; freedom and bliss should belong to this subject as predicates. Although for the neo-Platonists, too, pagan virtue was still truth—hence the distinction from Christian theology that transferred the bliss, perfection, and the divine likeness of man to the other world—this predicate becomes a subject; that is, an adjective of man becomes a substantive, a real being. Precisely in this manner, real man became also a mere abstraction without flesh and blood, an allegorical figure of the divine being. Plotinus, at least according to the report of his biographer, was ashamed to have a body.

30

The statement that only the "concrete" notion that carries the nature of the real in itself is the true notion expresses the recognition of the truth of concreteness or reality. But because simultaneously the notion—that is, the essence of thought—is presupposed from the start as the absolute and only true being, the real or actual can be recognized only in an indirect way and only as the essential and necessary adjective of the notion. Hegel is a realist, but a purely idealistic realist or, rather, an abstract realist; he is a realist in the abstraction from all reality. He negates thought, namely, abstract thought; but the negation is itself within abstract thought so that the negation of abstraction is itself an abstraction. According to Hegel, philosophy has for an object only "that which is"; but this "is" is itself only an abstracted and ideated "is." Hegel is a thinker who surpasses himself in thought; he wants to grasp the thing itself, but in the thought of the thing. He wants to be apart from thought, but within thought itself —hence the difficulty in comprehending the "concrete" notion.

31

The recognition of the light of reality in the darkness of abstraction is a contradiction; it is the affirmation of the real in its negation. The new philosophy is the philosophy that thinks of the concrete not in an abstract, but in a concrete manner. It is the philosophy that recognizes the real in its reality as true, namely, in a manner corresponding to the essence of the real, and raises it into the principle and object of philosophy. The new philosophy is, therefore, the truth of the Hegelian philosophy and of modern philosophy in general.

The following is a more precise deduction of the historical necessity or genesis of the new philosophy from the old philosophy. According to Hegel, the concrete notion, the idea, is at first only abstract and only in the element of thought; it is the rationalized God of theology before the creation of the world. But, as God manifests, reveals, temporalizes, and actualizes himself, so does the idea realize itself; Hegel is the history of theology transformed into a logical process. Once we arrive, however, with the realization of the idea in the realm of realism, and the truth of the idea is that it is real and that it exists, then we have indeed in existence the criterion of truth: only that which is real is true. And now questions present themselves. What is real? That which is only thought of? That which is only an object of thought and mind. But in this way we will not extricate ourselves from the idea *in abstracto*. An object of thought is also the Platonic idea; an inner object is also the heavenly other world that is an object of faith and imagination. If the reality of thought is ideated reality, then the reality of thought is itself only an idea, and we remain forever in the identity of thought with itself, in idealism. It is an idealism that differentiates itself from subjective idealism only in that it embraces the total content of reality, making it a determinateness of thought. If there is, therefore, real seriousness about the reality of thought or the idea, then something other than itself must be added to it or, the idea as a realized idea must be other than unrealized, as a mere idea; it must be an object, not only for thinking, but also for not-thinking. The self-realization of the idea means that it negates itself and ceases to be a mere idea. What is then this not-thinking, that which is differentiated from thinking? It is the sensuous. The self-realization of the idea means, accordingly, that it makes itself into an object of the senses. The reality of the idea is thus sensation. But reality is the truth of the idea; thus, sensation is the truth of the idea. Precisely so we managed to make sensation a predicate and the idea or thought a subject. But why, then, does the idea represent itself in sensation? Why is it not true when it is not real, that is, sensuous? Is not its truth made, therefore, dependent on sensation? Is not meaning and worth granted to the sensuous for itself, disregarding the fact that it is the reality of the idea? If sensation for itself is nothing, of what need is it to the idea? If only the idea gives value and content to sensation, then sensation is a pure luxury and a trifle; it is only an illusion that the idea presents to itself. But it is not so. The idea is required to realize itself and represent itself in sensation only because, unknowing to the idea, reality and sensation, independent of the idea, are presupposed as the truth. The idea proves its worth through sensation; how would this be possible if sensation were not unconsciously accepted as the truth? Because, however, one starts consciously with the truth of the idea, the truth of sensation is expressed only afterward, and sensation is made only into an attribute of the idea. This is, however, a contradiction, for it is only an attribute and still it gives truth to the idea; namely, it is simultaneously the main thing and an accessory, essence and accident. We save ourselves from this contradiction only if we make the real, that is, the sensuous, into its own subject and give it an absolutely independent, divine, and primary meaning which is not first derived from the idea.

32

The real in its reality or taken as real is the real as an object of the senses; it is the sensuous. Truth, reality, and sensation are identical. Only a sensuous being is a true and real being. Only through the senses, and not through thought for itself, is an object given in a true sense. The object that is given in thought or that is identical with thought is only idea.

Namely, a real object is given to me only where a being that affects me is given to me and where my self-activity—when I start from the viewpoint of thought—finds its boundary or resistance in the activity of another being. The notion of the object is originally nothing other than the notion of another "I"; thus, man in his childhood comprehends all things as freely active and arbitrary beings; therefore, the notion of the object is generally mediated by the notion of the "thou," of the objectified "I." An object, that is, another "I," is given—to speak in Fichtean language—not to the "I," but to the "not-I" in me; for only where I am transformed from an "I" into a "thou," where I am passive, does the conception of an activity existing apart from me, that is, objectivity, arise. But only through the senses is an "I" a "not-I."

The following question is characteristic for the abstract philosophy of earlier times: How can different and independent beings, that is, substances, affect one another? For example, how can the body affect the soul, that is, the "I"? This question was, however, insoluble for them because it was abstracted from sensation and because the substances, which were to affect one another, were abstract beings, pure entities of the mind. The secret of the reciprocal effect is solved only by sensation. Only sensuous beings affect one another. I am an "I" for myself and simultaneously a "thou" for others. This I am, however, only as a sensuous being. The abstract mind, nevertheless, isolates this being-for-itself as substance, atom, "I," or God. It can, therefore, only arbitrarily connect the being-for-others with the being-for-itself; for the necessity of this connection is only sensation, from which, however, the mind abstracts. That of which I think without sensation I think of without and apart from all connection. How can I, therefore, think at the same time of the unconnected as connected?

33

The new philosophy regards and considers being as it is for us, not only as thinking but as really existing beings; thus, it regards being as an object of being, as an object of itself. Being as an object of being—and only this being is being and deserves the name of being—is the being of the senses, perception, feeling, and love. Being is thus a secret of perception, of feeling, and of love.

Only in feeling and in love does "this"—as in "this person" or "this object," that is, the particular—have absolute value and is the finite the infinite; in this alone, and only in this, is the infinite depth, divinity, and truth of love constituted. Only in love is God—who counts the hair on one's head—truth and reality. The Christian God is himself only an abstraction of human love and an image of it. But, precisely because "this" has absolute value only in love, the secret of being discloses itself only in it and not in abstract thought. Love is passion, and only passion is the hallmark of existence. Only that exists which is an object—be it real or possible—of passion. Abstract thought that is without feeling and without passion cancels the difference between being and nonbeing, but this difference—which for thought is an evanescent difference—is a reality for love. Love means nothing other than becoming aware of this difference. To him who loves nothing

—let the object be whatever one wishes—it is all the same whether something does or does not exist. But, by the same token, as being in distinction from nonbeing is given to me only through love and feeling generally, so also is an object in distinction from me given to me only through love. Pain is a loud protest against the identification of the subjective with the objective. The pain of love means that that which is in the imagination is not in reality. The subjective is here the objective, and the imagination is the object; but this ought not to be. This is a contradiction, a falsehood, and a misfortune; hence the longing for the restoration of the true relationship, where the subjective and objective are not identical. Even physical pain expresses this difference evidently enough. The pain of hunger is due only to the fact that there is no object in the stomach; thus the stomach is, as it were, an object to itself, and the empty walls rub against one another instead of against some other substance. Hence, human feelings have no empirical or anthropological significance in the sense of the old transcendent philosophy; they have ontological and metaphysical significance. In feelings—indeed, in the feelings of daily occurrence—the deepest and highest truths are concealed. Thus, love is the true ontological proof of the existence of an object apart from our mind; there is no other proof of being but love and feeling in general. That object whose being affords you pleasure and whose nonbeing affords you pain—that alone exists. The distinction between object and subject, between being and nonbeing, is a distinction just as pleasing as it is painful.

34

The new philosophy rests on the truth of love and feeling. In love and in feeling generally, every man confesses the truth of the new philosophy. The new philosophy itself is basically nothing other than the essence of feeling elevated to consciousness; it only affirms in reason and with reason what every man—the real man—professes in his heart. It is the heart made into mind. The heart does not want abstract, metaphysical, or theological objects; it wants real and sensuous objects and beings.

35

Whereas the old philosophy said, "that which is not thought of does not exist," so does the new philosophy, on the other hand, say, "that which is not loved and cannot be loved does not exist." That, however, which cannot be loved also cannot be worshiped. Only that which can be an object of religion is an object of philosophy.

Love is objectively as well as subjectively the criterion of being, of truth, and of reality. Where there is no love, there is also no truth. And only he who loves something is something; to be nothing and to love nothing are identical. The more one is, the more one loves, and vice versa.

36

Whereas the old philosophy started by saying, "I am an abstract and merely a thinking being to whose essence the body does not belong," the new philosophy, on the other hand, begins by saying, "I am a real, sensuous being and, indeed, the body in its totality is my ego, my essence itself." The old philosopher was thinking, therefore, in continuous contradiction and quarrel with the senses in order to repel the sensuous conceptions from soiling the abstract notions; the new philosopher, on the other hand, thinks in harmony and peace with the senses. The old philosophy confessed the truth of sensation even in the notion of God who comprehends being in himself; for this being was, indeed, supposed to be at the same time a being distinct from being thought, a being apart from mind and thought, a real, objective, that is, sensuous being; it was confessed only in a manner that was hidden, conceptual, unconscious, and reluctant, solely because it was coerced. The new philosophy, on the other hand, recognizes the truth of sensation with joy and consciousness; it is the open-hearted and sensuous philosophy.

37

Modern philosophy searched for something immediately certain. It rejected, therefore, the thinking of the scholastics which was groundless and unfounded and founded philosophy on self-consciousness; that is, it set the thinking being, the ego, and the self-conscious mind in the place of the merely ideated being, in place of God, who is the highest and last being of all scholastic philosophy; for thought is infinitely closer, more present, and certain to the thinking person than is the thought-of. The existence of God is doubtful, and so is generally that which I think; but that I exist, that is, I who think and doubt, is certain. But the self-consciousness of modern philosophy is itself in turn only a being ideated and mediated through abstraction and thus a doubtful being. Certain and immediately assured is only that which is an object of the senses, perception, and feeling.

38

The true and divine is only that that needs no proof, that is certain directly in itself, that directly speaks for itself and convinces in itself, and in which the affirmation that it exists is directly implied; it is that that is plainly decided upon, that is certain and clear as daylight. But only the sensuous is clear as daylight; all doubt and dispute cease only where sensation begins. The secret of immediate knowledge is sensation.

All is mediated, says the Hegelian philosophy. Something is true, however, only when it is no longer mediated, but immediate. Historical epochs arise, therefore, only where that which before was only ideated and mediated becomes an object of immediate and sensuous certainty, namely, that which before was only idea becomes truth. It is scholasticism to make mediation into a divine necessity and an essential attribute of truth. Its necessity is merely a conditional necessity; it is necessary only where a false presupposition still forms the basis, where a truth or a doctrine presents itself in contradiction to a doctrine that is also still taken as true and is respected. The self-mediated truth is the truth that is still attached to its opposite statement. One starts with the opposite statement which, however, is afterward sublated. If, however, the opposite statement is one that is to be sublated and negated, why should I begin with it and not immediately with its negation? Let us take an example. God as God is an abstracted being; he particularizes, determines, and realizes himself in the world and in man; thus, he is concrete and thus, at first, is the abstract being negated. But why should I not then start immediately with the concrete? Why should not that which is certain and proven valid through itself be higher than that which is certain through the negation of its contrary? Who can elevate mediation to necessity and to a law of truth? Only he who himself is still imprisoned by that which is to be negated, who still struggles and quarrels with himself, and who still has not completely made up his mind; in short, only he in whom truth is only talent, a matter of special, even outstanding, ability but not genius and a matter of the whole man. Genius is immediate, sensuous knowledge. What talent has only in the head genius has in the flesh and blood; namely, that which for talent is still an object of thought is for genius an object of the senses.

39

The old absolute philosophy banished the senses to the realm of appearance and finiteness; and yet, in contradiction to this, it determined the absolute, the divine, as the object of art. But the object of art is—mediated in literature and immediate in the visual arts—an object of seeing, hearing, and feeling. Thus, not only the finite and appearing but also the true and divine being is an object of the senses; namely, sense is an organ of the absolute. Art "depicts the truth in sensation"; this means, when rightly comprehended and expressed, that art depicts the truth of sensation.

40

Just as in art, so it is in religion. Sensuous perception, and not the imagination, is the essence of the Christian religion; it is the form and organ of the highest and divine being. Where, however, sensuous perception is taken as the organ of the divine and true being, there the divine being is expressed and recognized as the sensuous being and the sensuous, as the divine being; for, as the subject is, so is the object.

"And the word became flesh and dwelt among us, and we saw its glory." Only for later generations is the object of the Christian religion an object of the imagination and of fantasy; but the original view is restored again. In Heaven, Christ, that is, God, is an object of immediate and sensuous perception; there he is transformed from an object of the imagination and of thought, hence from a spiritual being which he is for us here, into a sensuous, perceptible, and visible being. And this perception is the beginning as well as the end, thus the essence, of Christianity. Speculative philosophy has, therefore, grasped and presented art and religion not in the true light, in the light of reality, but rather only in the twilight of reflection, in that it dissolved sensation—in pursuance of its principle, which is abstraction from sensation—into a mere form-determination of art and religion; art is God in the form-determination of sensuous perception, and religion is God in the form-determination of the imagination. In truth, however, only that which appears to reflection as the form is the essence. Where God appears in the fire and is worshiped, there, in truth, the fire is worshiped as God. God in the fire is nothing other than the essence of fire which, because of its effects and attributes, astounds man; God in man is nothing other than the essence of man. Just so, that which art depicts in the form of sensation is nothing other than the very essence of sensation that is inseparable from this form.

41

Not only "external" things are objects of the senses. Man is given to himself only through the senses; he is an object of himself only as an object of the senses. The identity of subject and object, which in self-consciousness is only an abstract idea, is truth and reality only in man's sensuous perception of man.

We feel not only stones and lumber, flesh and bones; we also feel feelings, in that we press the hands or lips of a feeling being; we hear through our ears not only the rustle of water and the whisper of leaves, but also the soulful voice of love and wisdom; we see not only mirror surfaces and colored spectres, but we also catch a man's glance. Thus, not only the external but also the internal, not only flesh but also mind, not only the object but also the ego are objects of the senses. Everything is, therefore, sensuously perceptible, and although not always immediately so, yet it is perceived through mediation. Although it is not always perceptible through the vulgar and crude senses or through the eyes of the anatomists or chemists, yet it is perceptible through the refined senses or through the eyes of the philosophers. Thus, empiricism rightly derives the origin of our ideas from the senses; only it forgets that the most important and essential sense object of man is man himself; it forgets that only in man's glimpse into man is the light of consciousness and understanding kindled. Idealism is, therefore, in the right when it looks for the origin of the ideas in man; but it is in the wrong when it wants to derive them from the isolated man determined as soul and as a being existing for itself, in short, when it wants to derive them from the "I" without a given sensuous "thou." Only through communication and conversation between man and man do the ideas arise. Not alone, but only with others, does one reach notions and reason in general. Two human beings are needed for the generation of man—of the spiritual as well as of the physical man; the community of man with man is the first principle and criterion of truth and generality. The certainty of the existence of other things apart from me is mediated for me through the certainty of the existence of another human being apart from me. That which I alone perceive I doubt; only that which the other also perceives is certain.

42

The differences between essence and appearance, ground and consequence, substance and accident, necessity and chance, speculative and empirical, do not constitute two realms or worlds of which one is a supersensuous world to which essence belongs and the other is a sensuous world to which appearance belongs; rather, these distinctions all fall within the realm of sensation itself.

Let us take an example from the natural sciences. In the Linnaean botanical system, the first classes are determined by the number of filaments. But already in the eleventh class where twelve to twenty stamens appear—and even more in the class of twenty stamens and of polystamens—the numerical determination becomes irrelevant; it is no longer enumerated. Here we have, therefore, before our eyes in one and the same realm the difference between determined and undetermined, between necessary and irrelevant, rational and irrational plurality. Thus, we need not go beyond sensation in order to reach the boundary of the merely sensuous and empirical in the sense of absolute philosophy; indeed, we must not separate the mind from the senses in order to find the supersensuous, that is, mind and reason, in the sensuous.

43

The sensuous is not, in the sense of speculative philosophy, the immediate; namely, it is not the profane, obvious, and thoughtless that is understood by itself. Immediate, sensuous perception comes much later than the imagination and the fantasy. The first perception of man is merely the perception of the imagination and of the fantasy. The task of philosophy and of science in general consists, therefore, not in leading away from sensuous, that is, real, objects, but rather in leading toward them, not in transforming objects into ideas and conceptions, but rather in making visible, that is, in objectifying, objects that are invisible to ordinary eyes.

Men first see the objects only as they appear to them and not as they are; they do not see themselves in the objects, but only their imaginations of the objects; they posit their own essence in them and do not differentiate the object from the conception of it. The imagination lies closer to the uneducated and subjective man than does intuition, for in intuition he is torn away from himself, whereas in the imagination he remains within himself. But as it is with the imagination, so it is with thought. Men will sooner, and for a much longer time, occupy themselves with heavenly and divine matters than with earthly and human things; that is, sooner and for much longer will they occupy themselves with things translated into ideas than with things in the original and primary language. Only now, in the modern era, has mankind arrived again—as once in Greece after the demise of the Oriental dream world—at the sensuous, that is, the unfalsified and objective perception of the sensuous, that is, of the real; precisely with this, however, it also came to itself; for a man who devotes himself only to entities of the imagination or of abstract thought is himself only an abstract or fantastic, but not a real and true human being. The reality of man depends only on the reality of his object. If you have nothing, you are nothing.

44

Space and time are not mere forms of appearance; they are conditions of being, forms of reason, and laws of existence as well as of thought.

To-be-here is the primary being, the primary determination. Here I am—this is the first sign of a real, living being. The index finger is the signpost from nothingness to being. Here is the first boundary and separation. Here am I, and you are there; we are apart from each other; hence, we can both exist without encroaching on the other; there is room enough. The sun is not where Mercury is, and Mercury is not where Venus is; the eye is not where the ear is; and so on. Where there is no space, there is also no room for any system. The determination of place is the first determination of reason on which every subsequent determination can rest. With the division into different places—and, with space, different places are immediately posited—organized nature begins. Reason orients itself only in space. "Where am I?" is the question of awakening consciousness and the first question of "the wisdom of life." Limitation in space and time is the first virtue, and difference in place is the first difference between that which is decent and that which is indecent. It is the first difference that we teach children, that is, undeveloped human beings, for whom the place is irrelevant, doing everything at every place without difference; so, too, does the fool. Fools, therefore, reach reason when they bind themselves again to a place and a time. To place different things in different places or to distinguish spatially what is qualitatively different is the condition for every economy, even for the spiritual economy. Not to put in the text what belongs in the footnote, not to put at the beginning what belongs at the end, in short, spatial separation and limitation belong also to the wisdom of the writer.

At any rate, we deal here always with a determined place; indeed, nothing more than the determination of a place is here taken into consideration. I cannot separate the place from space if I want to grasp space in its reality. With the question "Where?" the conception of space first arises for me. "Where?" is general and is valid without distinction for every place, and yet "where" is determined. With this "where," the other "where" is simultaneously posited; hence, with the determination of place, the generality of space is simultaneously posited.

But, precisely therefore, the general notion of space is a real and concrete notion only in connection with the determination of place. Hegel accords space, like nature generally, only a negative determination. But to-be-here is positive. I am not there because I am here; this not-being-there is thus only a consequence of the positive, expressive being-here. That here is not there, that one is apart from the other, is only a limit of your imagination, but not a limit in itself. It is a being apart that ought to be and that does not oppose but rather corresponds to reason. In Hegel, however, this being apart is a negative determination because it is the being apart of that which ought not to be apart, for the logical notion as the absolute identity with itself is taken as the truth! Space is, precisely therefore, the negation of the idea and of reason; hence, reason can be re-introduced into space only through its negation. But not only is space not the negation of reason, it provides place for reason and the idea; space is the first sphere of reason. Where there is no spatial being apart, there also is no logical being apart. Or vice versa—if we wish, like Hegel, to go from logic to space—where there is no distinction, there also is no space. Differences in thought must be realized as differentiated things—differentiated things, however, separate spatially from one another. Hence only spatial being apart is the truth of logical distinctions. But those things that are apart from one another can only be thought of one after the other. Real thinking is thinking in space and time. The very negation of space and time (duration of time) falls always within space and time. We wish to save space and time only in order to gain them.

45

Things must not be thought of otherwise than as they appear in reality. That which is separated in reality ought also not to be identical in thought. The exemption of thought and the idea—the world of intellect in neo-Platonism—from the laws of reality is the privilege of theological arbitrariness. The laws of reality are also the laws of thought.

46

The immediate unity of opposite determinations is only possible and valid in abstraction. In reality, opposite statements are always connected through an intermediary notion. This intermediary notion is both the object and the subject of the opposite statements.

Therefore, nothing is easier than to show the unity of opposite predicates; one need only abstract from the object or subject of the opposite statements. The boundary between the opposite statements vanishes with the object; they are now without a bottom and without support, and thus they immediately collapse together. If, for example, I regard being only as such and I abstract from every determination that exists, then of course being equals nothingness for me. The difference, the boundary, between being and nothingness is indeed only the determinant. When I omit that which exists, what is still this mere "is"? But what is valid for this antithesis and its identity is also valid for the identity of all the other antitheses of speculative philosophy.

47

The only means by which opposing and contradicting determinations are united in the same being in a way corresponding to reality is time.

This at least is the case with living beings. Only thus, for example in man, does the contradiction appear whereby I am now occupied and dominated by this determination—that is, this feeling or this intention—and now by another opposing determination. Only where one conception or one feeling displaces another, where no decision and no permanent determination is reached, and where the soul finds itself in a continu-

ous alternation of opposing states does the soul find itself in
the hellish pains of contradiction. Were I to unify simultaneously the opposing determinations within myself, they would
blunt and neutralize one another like the opposing elements
of a chemical process that exist simultaneously yet lose their
differences in a neutral product. The pain of contradiction
consists precisely in that I am and passionately wish to be now
that which in the next instant I, just as vigorously, am not and
wish not to be, in that affirmation and negation follow each
other, each excluding the other and each affecting me in its
full determination and sharpness.

48

The real can be presented in thought not by integers but
only by fractions. This difference is normal; it rests on the
nature of thought whose essence is generality, in distinction
from reality, whose essence is individuality. That this difference, however, does not culminate in an outright contradiction between the ideated and the real is only due to the fact
that thought does not follow a straight line in identity with
itself, but rather interrupts itself through sensuous perception.
Only that thought which is determined and rectified by sensuous perception is real and objective thought—the thought
of objective truth.

It is most important to recognize that absolute thought, that
is, isolated thought that is separated from sensation, will not
get beyond formal identity, namely, the identity of thought
with itself; for, although thought or the notion is determined
as the unity of opposing determinations, yet these determinations themselves are only abstractions and determinations of
ideas, and always identities of thought with itself, that is, only
multiples of the identity from which, as the absolute truth,
one had started. The other, which the idea posits as opposite
to itself, is—as one posited by the idea—not truly and really
distinct from the idea and apart from it; at most it is dis-

charged only *pro forma*, as appearance in order to show its liberality; for this otherness of the idea is itself again the idea, only not yet in the form of the idea, not yet posited and realized as idea. Thus, thought for itself alone cannot bring about any positive distinction and opposition to itself; but for this very reason it has also no criterion of truth other than that nothing should contradict the idea or thought; thus, it has only a formal and subjective criterion that does not decide whether the ideated truth is also a real truth. The criterion that decides this is solely perception. One ought, indeed, always to listen to the opponent. But it is precisely sensuous perception that is the opponent of thought. Perception takes matters in a broad sense, whereas thought takes them in a narrow sense. Perception leaves matters in their unlimited freedom, whereas thought gives them laws, which, however, are only too often despotic. Perception enlightens the mind, but determines and decides nothing; thought determines but also often narrows the mind. Perception for itself has no principles, whereas thought for itself no life. The rule is the concern of thought, whereas the exception to the rule is the concern of perception. Hence, just as only perception that is determined by thought is true perception, so conversely only thought that is broadened and opened by perception is true thought corresponding to the essence of reality. Thought that is continuous and identical with itself lets the world, in contradiction with reality, circle around its center; thought, however, that is interrupted by the observation of the disproportion of this movement, hence, by the anomaly of perception, transforms according to truth this circle into an ellipse. The circle is the symbol and the coat of arms of speculative philosophy, of thought which rests on itself; Hegel's philosophy, too, as is well known, is a circle of circles, although with regard to the planets it posits the orbit—but only because it is compelled to by experience—as "the path of a badly uniform movement"; the ellipse, on the other hand, is the symbol and coat of arms of sensuous philosophy, of thought that rests on perception.

truth, of the whole man. Or, to put it in another way, the new philosophy does indeed rest also on reason, but on that reason whose essence is the human being; namely, it rests not on a beingless, colorless, and nameless reason, but on reason saturated with the blood of man. Hence, whereas the old philosophy declared that only the rational is the true and real, the new philosophy, on the other hand, declares that only the human is the true and real, for only the human is the rational; man is the measure of reason.

51

The unity of thought and being has meaning and truth only when man is comprehended as the ground and subject of this unity. Only a real being recognizes real objects; only where thought is not the subject of itself but a predicate of a real being is the idea not separated from being. The unity of thought and being is, therefore, not formal, so that being would belong to thought in and for itself as a determination; it depends only on the object, the content of thought.

From this result the following categorical imperatives: Desire not to be a philosopher, as distinct from a man; be nothing else than a thinking man. Do not think as a thinker, that is, with a faculty torn from the totality of the real human being and isolated for itself; think as a living and real being, as one exposed to the vivifying and refreshing waves of the world's oceans. Think in existence, in the world as a member of it, not in the vacuum of abstraction as a solitary monad, as an absolute monarch, as an indifferent, superworldly God; then you can be sure that your ideas are unities of being and thought. How should thought as the activity of a real being not grasp real objects and beings? Only when thought is separated from man and is determined for itself alone do awkward, fruitless, and, from this viewpoint, insoluble questions arise. How does thought arrive at being, that is, at the object? For thought determined for itself alone, that is, posited apart from man, is apart from all ties and connections to the world. You elevate yourself to an object only by lowering yourself to be an object for others. You think only because your ideas themselves can be thought, and they are true only when they pass the test of objectivity, that is, when they are acknowledged by another person apart from you for whom they are an object. You see only as you yourself are a visible being, and you feel only as you yourself are a perceptible being. The world stands open only to an open mind, and the openings of the mind are the senses only. But that thought that is isolated for itself, enclosed in itself, without senses, without and apart from man, is absolute subject that cannot be and ought not be an object for others; for this very reason, however, it will also never find—despite all efforts—a transition to the object and to being; its likelihood is as small as that of a head separated from the body finding a transition by which it can get hold of an object, the reason being that the means, that is, the organs, to do so are lacking.

52

The new philosophy is the complete and absolute dissolution, without any contradiction, of theology into anthropology; for it is the dissolution of theology not only in reason—as was the case in the old philosophy—but also in the heart, in short, in the whole and real being of man. In this respect, the new philosophy is only the necessary result of the old philosophy, for that which was once dissolved in the mind must finally dissolve itself also in the life, heart, and blood of man; but it is also at the same time the truth of the old philosophy and, indeed, a new and independent truth, for only the truth that became flesh and blood is the truth. The old philosophy necessarily reverted to theology; that which is sublated only in the mind and in the notion has still an antithesis in the heart. The new philosophy, on the other hand, can never relapse; that which is dead in both body and soul can never return, not even as a ghost.

53

Man distinguishes himself from the animals not only by thinking. His whole being, rather, constitutes his distinction from the animals. To be sure, he who does not think is not a man; not however, because thinking is the cause, but only because it is a necessary consequence and attribute of the human essence.

So we need not also here reach beyond the realm of sensation in order to recognize man as a being ranking above the animals. Man is not a particular being, like the animals, but a universal being; he is not, then, a limited and restricted being, but rather an unlimited and free being, for universality, absoluteness, and freedom are inseparable. This freedom does not lie in a special faculty, that is, will, nor does universality lie in a special faculty of thinking, that is, reason; this freedom and this universality extend themselves over man's total being. The senses of the animal are indeed keener than those of man, but only in respect to certain objects that necessarily relate to the needs of the animal; and they are keener precisely because of this determination, this excluding limitation to a definite object. Man does not have the sense of smell of a hunting dog or of a raven, but only because his sense of smell is a sense embracing all kinds of smell; hence it is a freer sense which, however, is indifferent to particular smells. But, wherever a sense is elevated above the limits of particularity and its bondage to needs, it is elevated to an independent and theoretical significance and dignity; universal sense is understanding; universal sensation, mind. Even the lowest senses, smell and taste, elevate themselves in man to intellectual and scientific acts. The smell and taste of things are objects of natural science. Indeed, even the stomach of man, which we view so contemptuously, is not animal but human because it is a universal being that is not limited to certain kinds of food. Precisely thereby is man free of the frenzy of voracity with which an animal throws itself over its prey. Leave man his head but give him the stomach of a lion or a horse, and he certainly will cease to be a man. A limited stomach conforms only to a limited, that is, animal, sense. The moral and rational relationship of man to the stomach consists therefore of treating the stomach, not as an animal being, but as a human being. He who concludes his view of man with the stomach, placing it in the class of animals, also consigns man, as far as eating is concerned, to bestiality.

54

The new philosophy makes man—with the inclusion of nature as the foundation of man—the unique, universal and highest object of philosophy. It thus makes anthropology, with the inclusion of physiology, the universal science.

55

Art, religion, philosophy, and science are only manifestations or revelations of the true human essence. Man, the complete and true man, is only he who possesses a sense that is esthetic or artistic, religious or moral, philosophic or scientific; in general, only he who excludes from himself nothing essentially human is man. "Homo sum, humani nihil a me alienum puto"—this sentence, taken in its most universal and highest meaning, is the motto of the new philosophy.

56

The absolute philosophy of identity has completely displaced the viewpoint of truth. The natural viewpoint of man, the viewpoint of the distinction between I and thou, subject and object, is the true and absolute viewpoint; consequently, it is also the viewpoint of philosophy.

57

The unity of mind and heart, according to the truth, consists, not in extinguishing or glossing over their difference, but rather only in that the essential object of the heart is also the essential object of the mind; namely, it consists only in the identity of the objects. The new philosophy—which makes the essential and highest object of the heart and of man likewise the most essential and highest object of the mind—thus establishes a rational unity of mind and heart, of thought and life.

58

Truth does not exist in thought for itself or in knowledge for itself. Truth is only the totality of human life and of the human essence.

59

The single man for himself possesses the essence of man neither in himself as a moral being nor in himself as a thinking being. The essence of man is contained only in the community and unity of man with man; it is a unity, however, which rests only on the reality of the distinction between I and thou.

60

Solitude is finiteness and limitation; community is freedom and infinity. Man for himself is man (in the ordinary sense); man with man—the unity of I and thou—is God.

61

The absolute philosopher said, or at least thought, of

himself—of course as a thinker and not as man—*La vérité c'est moi,* in a way similar to the saying, *L'état c'est moi* of the absolute monarch, and the saying, *L'être c'est moi* of the absolute God. The human philosopher, on the other hand, says: even in thinking and in being a philosopher, I am a man among men.

62

The true dialectic is not a monologue of a solitary thinker with himself; it is a dialogue between I and thou.

63

The Trinity was the highest mystery and the focal point of absolute philosophy and religion. But as was historically and philosophically shown with regard to the essence of Christianity, the secret of the Trinity is the secret of communal and social life; it is the secret of the necessity of the "thou" for an "I"; it is the truth that no being—be it man, God, mind, or ego—is for itself alone a true, perfect, and absolute being, that truth and perfection are only the connection and unity of beings equal in their essence. The highest and last principle of philosophy is, therefore, the unity of man with man. All essential relations—the principles of various sciences—are only different kinds and ways of this unity.

64

The old philosophy possesses a double truth—the truth for itself, which was not concerned with man, that is, philosophy, and the truth for man, that is, religion. The new philosophy, on the other hand, as the philosophy of man is also essentially the philosophy for man; it possesses an essentially practical—and indeed in the highest sense practical—tendency without damaging the dignity and independence of theory, indeed in closest harmony with it. It takes the place of religion and has the essence of religion within itself. In truth, it is itself religion.

65

So far, the attempts at philosophical reform have differed more or less from the old philosophy only in form, but not in substance. The indispensable condition of a really new philosophy, that is, an independent philosophy corresponding to the needs of mankind and of the future, is, however, that it will differentiate itself in its essence from the old philosophy.

Index

Abstraction: concreteness from, 44; of God, 46; man and, 48; negation of, 48 − 49; from object, 19; problem of, xxvii, from sensation, 13, 30 − 32, 51 − 52

Accident: substance and, 16, 59

Action: God as, 12, 18 − 19

Alienation: of man from essence, 37; of self, xxvii; of spirit, 32; theory of, xviii

Animals: man distinguished from, 69 − 70; object of, 9 − 10

Anthropologism, viii, xvii, xix, xxvii *n*.

Anthropology, philosophical, 3, 23; ancient philosophy, 45; dissolution of theology into, 5, 68

Anthropology, Christology, 5

Apotheosis: of reason, 26

Appearance: accepted by sense perception, 34 − 35; essence and, 59; reality and, 62

Aquinas, St. Thomas, 16

Aristotle, 45

Art: sensation and, 57 − 58. *See also* Music; Poetry

Atheism: xviii, materialistic, 22; negation of, 33; partial, 24; philosophic, 19, 25; of senses, 30

Being, criteria of, 54; equal, 10; essence and, 9, 15; extended, 22 − 23; imperfection of, 72; ineffability of, 44; mind and, 20 − 21, 30; nothingness and, 40 − 42, 61, 63; object and, 19, 52; reason and, 6 − 7, 46. *See also* Existence; Individual being; Man

Being, divine. *See* Divinity; God

Being, thought and, 38 − 48; absolute being and absolute thought, 12; contradiction, 42 − 43; Descartes' *cogito*, 31; identity, 38; neo-Platonic position, 44 − 48; unity, 67 − 68

Belief in God. *See* Faith

Berkeley, George, xxiiff.

Bliss, neo-Platonic concept of, 48. *See also* Rapture

Buber, Martin, viii

Cartesian philosophy. *See* Descartes

Cause: of evil, 25, 37; God as, 13, 20, 22

Chance, 59. *See also* Accident

Change: necessity for, 25

Christian theology, 33, 48

Christianity, 5; essence of, ix, xivff. xvi, 57, 72; Hegel's attempt to restore Christianity, 34; theoretical negation of, 25

Circle as symbol of absolute thought, 1, 65

Communication, 58. *See also* Language

Community, xvi, xxix, 58 − 59; truth in, 17, 71

Concreteness, 56; from abstractness, 44; Hegel's concept of, 1, 49; as predicate of thought, 46 − 47; true reality, in 48. *See also* Reality

Consciousness: essence of feeling elevated to, 53; existence and, 27 − 28; of self, 55, 58

Creation: divine, 11 − 12, 20; of God in imagination, 6